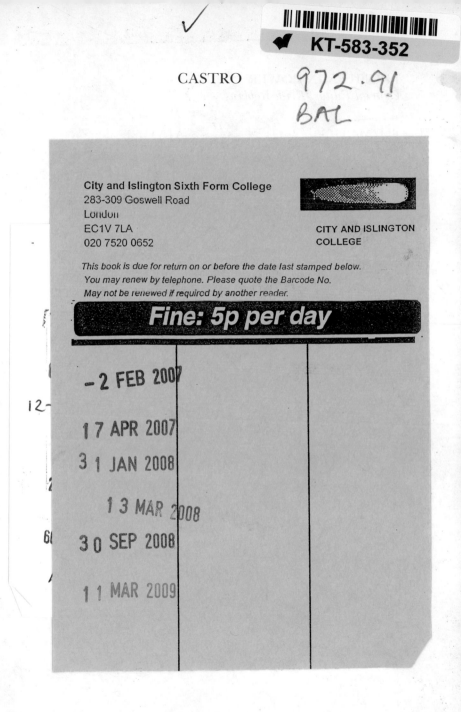

KT-583-352

CASTRO 972.91
BAL

City and Islington Sixth Form College
283-309 Goswell Road
London
EC1V 7LA
020 7520 0652

CITY AND ISLINGTON
COLLEGE

This book is due for return on or before the date last stamped below.
You may renew by telephone. Please quote the Barcode No.
May not be renewed if required by another reader.

Fine: 5p per day

- 2 FEB 2007

1 7 APR 2007

3 1 JAN 2008

1 3 MAR 2008

3 0 SEP 2008

1 1 MAR 2009

. . . .

CASTRO

SECOND EDITION

Sebastian Balfour

LONGMAN
London and New York

Longman Group Limited,
Longman House, Burnt Mill,
Harlow, Essex CM20 2JE, England
and Associated Companies throughout the world.

*Published in the United States of America
by Longman Publishing, New York*

©Longman Group UK Limited 1990
This edition © Longman Group Limited 1995

First published 1990
Second edition 1995

ISBN 0 582 245583 PPR

British Library Cataloguing-in-Publication Data

A catalogue record for this book is
available from the British Library

Library of Congress Cataloging-in-Publication Data

Balfour, Sebastian.
 Castro / Sebastian Balfour. — 2nd ed.
  p. cm. — (Profiles in power)
 Includes bibliographical references and index.
 ISBN 0–582–25992–4 (pbk.)
 1. Castro, Fidel, 1927–   . 2. Cuba—Politics and
 government—1959–   3. Heads of state—Cuba—Biography. I. Title.
 II. Series: Profiles in power (London, England)
F1788.22.C3B35 1995
972.9106′4′092—dc20
[B]
                                                                94–36634
                                                                      CIP

Set by 5B in 10½ Baskerville Linotronic 202
Produced by Longman Singapore Publishers (Pte) Ltd.
Printed in Singapore

CONTENTS

PREFACE
TO THE FIRST EDITION

To set out to evaluate the career of a living statesman is always a hazardous venture; none more so than in the case of Fidel Castro. Though he has outlived almost every other head of state in the world, he is still relatively young and in full command of his senses. He has not said his last word on the international stage and he is likely to continue inspiring or dismaying politicians and people across the world. Any endeavour to interpret his political career faces two further problems: the hermeticism of the regime and Castro's own reticence about his private life. The processes of decision-making within the Cuban state are not open to public scrutiny so that the analysis of events and policies in Cuba has to rely to a great extent on deduction and inference. Castro has never discussed the intimate details of his life and has only on rare occasions talked about his childhood and youth, distrusting the tendency to personify political achievements.

Despite these obstacles a new study of Castro seems a compelling project. Over thirty years have passed since he took power and yet he remains something of an enigma to friend and foe alike. This is not through any shortage of interviews or biographical treatments. But the bibliography on Castro, with few exceptions, is as poor as it is prolific. There is a dearth of accounts dealing at any length with the last twenty years. Recent biographies of Castro have been long on anecdote and description but short on analysis. A revaluation of Castroism appears all the more timely in view of the fundamental changes taking place in the Soviet bloc at the instigation of Gorbachev.

In keeping with the series *Profiles in Power* of which it is part, this book is more an assessment of Castro's political ideas and sources of power than a biography, though personal details are included to the extent that they sustain the narrative and illuminate the subject. Within a chronological framework, the book sets out to examine the historical context in which Castro emerged as a national and international statesman and the ideological base on which the new Cuban state was founded. It attempts to analyze the changing structure of power in post-Revolutionary Cuba and stresses the Cuban and Third World dimension of Castroism.

The primary sources used in its preparation were mainly the words of Castro himself, of which there is no shortage, as well as letters and documents published in Cuba and elsewhere. However, the book does not set out to break new ground in research but rather to reinterpret the Castro phenomenon in the light of recent investigation; the monographs and academic articles on Cuba that have appeared in the last ten years or so have been an important source of information and analysis on this account. I am grateful to the Cuban historians, journalists, writers, and officials who kindly agreed to be interviewed by me during my visit in the summer of 1988, and to the librarians of the José Martí library in Havana who gave me access to its archives. I benefited from conversations with Peggy Gilpin, José Antonio Evora, Lynn Geldof, Tomás Gutiérrez Alea, Jorge Ibarra, Olga Cabrera, Luis Felipe Bernaza, Pablo Armando Fernández, and Ramon Fernández-Larrea. I am indebted to Marge Zimmerman for sharing with me her insights into contemporary Cuba. I owe a special debt of gratitude to Jean Stubbs who read through the manuscript and made invaluable suggestions. Neither she nor anyone else above is responsible for errors that may occur in this book nor for the nature of my interpretation of Castro and Castroism. Finally, I wish to thank my wife Gráinne Palmer for her unfailing encouragement and tolerance.

PREFACE
TO THE SECOND EDITION

Since the first edition of this book appeared, living conditions in Cuba have deteriorated to such an extent that it appears unthinkable to many that the Castro regime can survive in its present form for much longer. The riots that took place in the slums of old Havana on 5 August 1994 and the perilous flight of thousands of boat people towards Miami have revealed the depth of the social and economic crisis in Cuba. Yet the cry of 'Freedom!' that resounded during the riots was a sign not of a new political awareness among poor Cubans, as some prominent opponents of Castro have wishfully claimed, but of economic desperation. Cubans want to have a job, to satisfy their hunger and to buy consumer goods. Their immediate plight is no different from that of millions of poor in Haiti, Latin America and the rest of the Third World. When people go hungry, ideologies wither. The achievements in social justice, health care and education, on which the regime's legitimacy have depended, are fast disappearing in the crisis. Medicines are now scarce, there is virtually no fuel to bus children to school and those who lack access to dollars go hungry.

Nevertheless, there is still no sign that the regime is under any serious internal threat. Its resilience cannot be explained away simply by fear, superstition or state repression, nor indeed by Castro's statesmanship. It is true that he has once again been able to turn a crisis to his advantage. By turning on the tap of immigration through lifting obstacles to mass exodus, he has given discontent a safety-valve and forced the US administration to the negotiating table. He used this strategy successfully in 1980, embarrassing the

Carter government just as the recent exodus has severely discomforted President Clinton.

The survival of the Castro regime thus far is due above all to the continued strength of nationalism in Cuba, which owes much of its force to the implacable hostility of the US government. It is a far richer vein than the oil reserves which foreign companies are exploring off the Cuban coast and on which the regime is pinning many of its hopes.

This second edition of *Castro* is an extended and revised version of the first and brings the analysis of the Castro regime up to date in a new chapter, 'Socialism or Death!' which charts the response of the Casto regime to the challenges of the post-Comunist world. Nothing that has happened since the publication of the first edition has altered the analysis that underpinned it and, in particular, the self-evident notion, ignored by so many commentators, that events in Cuba can only be properly understood in the light of Cuban history.

September 1994

FOR ROSA AND MARIANNA

. . . . .

INTRODUCTION

The story of Fidel Castro can have few parallels in contemporary history. Most of the outstanding Third World leaders of this century like him emerged out of the anti-colonial struggles of the post-war period but none has played such a prominent and restless part on the international stage as Castro and none has survived as head of state for as long as he has done. It is difficult to think of many other political figures in the latter half of this century who have been so controversial and whose careers have touched on so many issues of global significance: Soviet-American relations, Third World nationalism, revolution and social justice in the south, war in Angola and Ethiopia, Third World debt, war and peace in Central America. Castro's rise to power in itself is an astonishing story of single-minded courage. With virtually no resources at first, he overthrew a US-backed military dictatorship and under the nose of the most powerful state in the world steered his small, Americanised island into Communist waters. For over thirty years, the US government has tried and failed to destroy his regime by subversion and coercion, by invasion by proxy and economic blockade. The two greatest powers in the world went to the brink of nuclear war over the right of Cuba to have nuclear missiles. Driven by the vision of one man, Cuba has become one of the best-educated and healthiest societies in the Third World. It is also one of the most militarised states in Latin America. A measure of its new power was the battle of Cuito Cuanavale in Angola in May 1988, when Cuban forces, backed by Angolan troops and closely monitored by their Commander-in-Chief, Castro, inflicted defeat on the South African army, forcing Pretoria to withdraw from Angola and negotiate the independence of Namibia.

1

The most striking feature of Cuba under Castro is the disproportion between its insignificant size and economic weight and the role that it has come to play in world affairs, at least until the late eighties. To find a comparable example, as one historian has pointed out, one has to look back to the Portuguese and Dutch empires of the seventeenth century or to eighteenth-century Britain.[1] Yet by any standard of probability the Cuban Revolution should have failed. For one, Castro should have been dead a long time before. As a student leader he survived numerous death threats and at least one assassination attempt. Almost all the outstanding radical leaders of his generation were gunned down by the police or by rivals. He should not have survived the bloody reprisals of the army after he and his followers had tried to seize a military barracks in 1953; most of his lieutenants were murdered in cold blood or tortured to death after their capture. He should not have escaped the military encirclement of his band of men after they had landed in nearly disastrous circumstances from a yacht in a swamp in a remote south-eastern corner of Cuba in 1956. Even subsequently, it should have been easy for the Cuban army to seek out his band and eliminate it. Taken out of context, moreover, Castro's whole revolutionary enterprise seems rather implausible. Both the attempt to launch a nation-wide rebellion in 1953 by trying to seize the military barracks of Moncada with a little over a hundred badly armed men, and his landing three years later with an even smaller force to overthrow the military regime appear foolhardy. The guerrilla campaign that followed the landing and led to the defeat of a US-backed army and air force seems a highly improbable endeavour. And that a small sugar island ninety miles from Florida and permeated by American culture should declare itself the first and only Communist state in the Western hemisphere seems bizarre in the extreme.

Yet the astonishing and unique process of the Cuban Revolution appears less incongruous in the light of Cuban history. Few of Castro's actions were without historical precedent. The attempted seizure of military barracks, the coastal landing in eastern Cuba, and the guerrilla campaign in the mountains of the East were all part of a long tradition in Cuba. The second and successful War of Independence against the Spanish, for example, had been launched in 1895 when its leaders had landed on hidden coves in the easternmost corner of Cuba. The subsequent guerrilla war had led to the defeat of the mighty army of the Spanish empire. Indeed, the degree to which the 1959 Revolution and Castro's career as a revolutionary leader echo the past is remarkable. Some of the parallels were the result of coincidence; many were due to similarity of conditions; and others were consciously sought by Castro himself. The popularity of Castro can be attributed to a great extent to the fact that he came to symbolise for many Cubans a long-cherished hope of national liberation and social justice. When a dove alighted on his shoulder as he made his victory speech in Havana in 1959 (there is no reason to suppose that it had been trained to do so) the illusion was complete; it must have seemed to many there that Castro was predestined to realise the long-frustrated aspirations of almost a hundred years of struggle. And indeed one gets the sense from some orthodox accounts of the Revolution that all happened as it was supposed to. Unable to understand the historical forces at work in the Revolution, even the CIA fell victim to theories of magic. Among the more exotic of their many abortive attempts to eliminate Castro was a plot to get his beard to fall out by having a CIA agent dust his shoes with the drug thalium, on the grounds, presumably, that his success lay in his charisma and his charisma lay in his beard. Even more far-fetched was a scheme originally suggested by Ian Fleming, the creator of James Bond, at a dinner party with the Kennedys, to stage-manage the Second Coming of Christ in Cuba. According to Senate Select Committee hearings in 1975, the plan was to spread rumours around the island that the Saviour was about to return to earth to denounce Castro as an anti-Christ; on the appointed day, a bearded CIA frogman would emerge on a beach in Cuba claiming to be Christ while an American submarine would surface just over the horizon shooting star shells into the sky.[2]

If the Cuban Revolution is inconceivable without Castro, it is equally true that it succeeded as a result of a specific set of historical conditions. Historians have stressed the peculiar economic and social structure of Cuba, distorted by its uneven and dependent development.[3] The Revolution also owed its survival in the early years to the strategic position of Cuba, situated almost within sight of the coast of Florida and therefore a prize asset during the expansionist administration of Khrushchev. The subsequent economic and military aid of the Soviet Union was essential in keeping the regime afloat and in allowing it to play a role in world affairs out of all proportion to its size. Since the collapse of Soviet and East European socialism, however, it has suffered a calamitous decline in both its economic health and its international status. Yet no structural or conjunctural factors can obscure the extraordinary individual role played by Castro in the history of Cuba since 1956. Any account of his career cannot fail also to be an interpretation of the Revolution itself. The central theme of this book, consequently, is the interaction between Castro's special qualities as a political leader (including his capacity to survive disaster through luck and determination) and the historical conditions that he and his supporters encountered and worked on.

. . .

NOTES AND REFERENCES

1. Hennessy A 1989 'The Cuban Revolution: a Wider View'. Paper to the Conference 'Cuba 30 Years On: the Dynamics of Change and the International Dimension', University of Warwick, 12–14 May 1989
2. Hinckle, Warren and Turner, William W 1981 *The Fish is Red. The Story of the Secret War against Castro*. Harper & Row, New York pp. 18 and 109–110. Also Bourne, Peter 1987 *Castro*. Macmillan, London, p. 212
3. For a brief survey of the historiography of the Cuban Revolution, see the Bibliographical essay on p. 171

Chapter 1

PICTURES OF THE PAST, VISIONS OF THE FUTURE

'Revolutionary governments are driven by pictures of the past as much as by visions of the future' Hugh Thomas, *Cuba: the Pursuit of Freedom*

When Fidel Castro entered the world of university politics in 1945 as a nineteen-year-old law student, two great historical events dominated the political rhetoric of his peers: the independence struggles of 1868 to 1898 and the revolutionary movement of 1927 to 1933 that had led to the overthrow of the dictator Machado. For student radicals, both events were interwoven into a picture of Cuban history as an incomplete and thwarted revolutionary process.

The largest island in the Caribbean, commanding the approaches north-west to the Gulf of Mexico and south to the Caribbean Sea, Cuba had been an important strategic centre of the Spanish empire in the New World. Almost twenty years before its conquest in 1511, Columbus had been struck by its beauty and also by its commercial potential. Topographically, Cuba is very varied. Three mountain ranges dominate the island, one in the centre and the others at its western and eastern ends, the tallest and most extensive being the Sierra Maestra in the east. Between the mountain ranges stretch wide and fertile plains on which are situated the main towns and where all but 5 per cent of the population live. The island's shoreline is also very diverse, from the low marshlands of part of the south-western coast to the mountains that rise sharply from the south-eastern shore. The coast is dotted with innumerable small natural harbours and a few miles offshore on each side of the island lie hundreds of tiny uninhabited islands and keys.

Under Spanish rule, Cuba had been dominated by the military, the clergy and the colonial administrators. Beneath this top echelon had been an elite of Cuban-born Spaniards or Creoles and much further down the social scale, the mulattos of mixed black and white race. The indigenous Indian population having been wiped out by conquest, disease and maltreatment, black slaves or ex-slaves occupied the bottom rung of this rigid hierarchy, providing the bulk of the labour force for the wealth that flowed to the metropolis from the sugar, tobacco and coffee plantations. Cuba thus became, in its racial mix, a typically Caribbean island, though with a stronger presence of whites than elsewhere in the area; in the 1980s 66 per cent of its population of 5.8 million were of European descent, 22 per cent were mulattos, and 12 per cent were black.

The Republic of Cuba had been born in 1902 after 400 years of colonisation by Spain. The battle for independence, waxing and waning for thirty years, had been a destructive and bloody affair, particularly in the final war of 1895–8; the toll it had taken of the male population was such that there were few men in their sixties when Castro's revolution took place in 1958.[1] It had also been a revolutionary struggle against slavery. The rank and file of the Cuban armies that threw themselves at the Spanish troops were black ex-slaves. A bitter war of attrition had been fought against the planters; many a former slave returned to burn down the canefields of his old master. In the first War of Independence, the mulatto general who led one of the armies, Antonio Maceo, had refused to enter into peace negotiations with the Spaniards unless they included the question of the abolition of slavery.

The struggle for independence had also been a fight against imperialism; Castro has on several occasions described Cuba as 'the nineteenth century's Vietnam'. Some of its leaders feared that once Cuba had broken away from Spain it would be swallowed up by the United States, which was at the time in a particularly expansionist mood. There had been talk earlier of the United States buying Cuba from Spain and some slave owners, looking towards the Confederate states in the South, had briefly flirted with the idea of its annexation by the United States because the Spanish government was tightening up its laws concerning slavery. In 1898, worried by the threat to North American assets of the continuing war in Cuba and determined to oust the old empire from the Caribbean, the United States declared war on Spain and after two months of hostilities forced it to give up its old and last colony. The new independent Cuba was thus born in the shadow of the eagle. Under the so-called Platt Amendment of 1901, the United States reserved to itself the right to intervene in the affairs of Cuba in order to prevent any other foreign power from exercising undue influence and to maintain 'stable government'. Despite this seemingly well-meaning paternalism, the four interventions by the US government between 1898 and 1920 were intended to ensure above all that Cuba maintained policies which favoured the increasing American investments on the island.

Indeed, it was US capital that re-colonised Cuba. Long before independence, giant American companies had moved in to exploit Cuba's natural resources. US investments on the island accelerated in the first quarter of the century and by 1926 were valued at $1,360 million, based in the sugar industry, and in railways, mining, tobacco, banking, commerce, real estate, and other sectors. US capital controlled the telephone service and the gas and electricity industries among others.[2] But it was sugar that set the tune in Cuba. Under a long-standing agreement, the United States committed itself to buying up to half of Cuba's sugar crop each year, thereby guaranteeing profits for the Cuban planters, foreign currency, and jobs. The Cuban sugar quota set by US Congress, however, was a mixed blessing because it meant that the United States could punish Cuba by reducing the price and amount of the quota if it stepped out of line. Thus the remaining Cuban sugar crop could be sold on the world market but only to the extent that it did not affect US sugar growers; otherwise, the sugar lobby on Capitol Hill would force down the quota. A Louisiana senator is reported in the Cuban press in 1955 to have made the following warning to the Cubans: 'I represent in the American Senate a vast sugar-producing area of the United States. And I have to demand here whatever benefits that area. . . . Cuba has exceeded its production [of sugar]. . . . It is we who permit your country to produce.'[3]

The United States also controlled Cuba's internal market. The Platt Amendment was replaced in 1934 by a more modern instrument of neo-colonial domination, the Reciprocal Trade Agreement, whereby in exchange for the sugar quota, US exports to Cuba were given preferential tariffs. The effect was to dampen any efforts at creating import substitution industries in Cuba and to discourage cheaper imports from elsewhere. The Agreement therefore served to lock Cuba's economy even more tightly into that of the United States. In 1957, another American senator called on Congress to lower the sugar quota because Cuba had just announced its intention to build two flour mills, thereby threatening the export of US flour to the island. A Cuban employers' review reacted sharply, stating in the conditional tense what was already a reality: 'Cuba would have to resign itself to having its economy "frozen" on the one hand by the limited US sugar quota and by world competition, and on the other by having to keep its internal market unchanged for the benefit of foreign exporters.'4

Any policy of developing Cuba's economy, any effort to regenerate Cuban society thus came to mean two related things in particular: to shake off its dependence on the United States, and to break out of the yoke of its sugar monoculture. Before the first marines landed in Cuba to supervise the new Republic, the so-called 'Apostle' of Cuban independence, the writer and poet José Martí, had warned against US expansionism. In a famous passage from his last and incomplete letter, written the day before he died in a cavalry charge against Spanish troops in 1895, Martí referred to the US as the 'monster': 'I have lived in the monster and I know its entrails: my sling is that of David.'5 Martí believed that the danger of US interference or aggression extended to the whole of the American continent south of the Rio Grande, to what he termed in his writings 'America'. 'The contempt of the formidable neighbour – who does not know it [America] – is the greatest danger facing our America, and it is vital, for visiting day is close by, that the neighbour gets to know it and gets to know it soon, so that it is not treated with contempt.'6 Martí feared above all that the United States would replace Spain as a colonial power in Latin America. More effectively than the old colonial power, however, the United States came to dominate the Cuban economy and that of many Latin American countries, shaping their societies and gearing their production to the demands of its own economy without permanently occupying their territories. As late as the early thirties, the dollar was the only paper currency in circulation in Cuba. The struggle for independence was seen by successive generations of radical young Cubans as unfinished business.

The Apostle Martí was an obligatory reference in the speeches of all political figures in the Cuban Republic, from generals to gangsters. But his official image was as a spiritual, millenarian patriot, free from any trace of anti-imperialism or rebelliousness. Such was the range of Martí's thought, expressed in poems, prose, newspaper articles, and letters, that it was possible to select different ideological messages to suit the circumstances. It was the student rebels of the twenties who rediscovered the radical Martí, and this alternative picture of the national hero was channelled through successive generations of students and left-wing leaders to the new university class of the forties.[7] Castro became one of the most dedicated disciples of Martí; the 'Apostle' became for the new aspiring liberator of Cuba a guide to action and a source of legitimacy. Castro never lost an opportunity to link himself publicly with the revolutionary traditions embodied by Martí, and in the darkest moments of his endeavour he was able to find some inspiration from the example of Martí's political labours. Imprisoned after his abortive attempt to storm the barracks of Moncada in 1953 and contemplating the seemingly impossible task of creating a revolutionary movement in Cuba, Castro wrote to a friend:

the similarity of situations reminds me of Martí's efforts to bring together all Cubans worthy of the fight for independence; each one had their history, their glories, their feats, each one believed they had more rights than or at least equal rights with the others; only the work of love, understanding and infinite patience of one man with less glory attached to him than others was able to achieve the miracle. . . . For this reason, perhaps, the pages of Cuban history I most admire are not to do with the heroic deeds on the battlefield but that gigantic, heroic and silent task of uniting Cubans for the struggle.[8]

In fact, striking parallels can be found between the lives of Martí and Castro. Both were sons of Spanish immigrants. Both were imprisoned for a while for their political activities on the same island, the Isle of Pines off the west coast of Cuba. Like Castro before his invasion of the island in 1956, Martí had raised money for his own expedition among Cuban exiles in Florida and on the Eastern seaboard of the United States. Martí had landed on a remote beach in eastern Cuba in difficult circumstances, though not as hazardous as those encountered by Castro about 288 kilometres further west some sixty-one years later. Indeed, the dictator Batista was so sure that Castro would take the same route as Martí that he ordered air surveillance missions on the southern coast of Oriente; in the event, the new would-be liberator landed on its western coast.[9] Castro's attempted seizure of the Moncada barracks in 1953 coincided with the much-publicised centenary of Martí's birth, allowing Castro to claim that he and his men, the 'generation of the centenary', were the true heirs of the 'Apostle'. Martí's party, the Cuban Revolutionary Party (PRC), like Castro's movement later, embraced radicals of different and in some measure contradictory political tendencies. Among the members of the PRC were socialist and anarcho-syndicalist workers, many of them immigrant tobacco workers living in Florida. A final, less important parallel was the use both Martí and Castro made of US journalists to publicise their cause whilst engaged in guerrilla warfare, Martí's champion being George Eugene Bryson of the *New York Herald* and Castro's Herbert L Matthews of the *New York Times*.

Martí represented a brand of romantic, republican nationalism that belonged to a very different period from that in which the young generation of the forties began their political careers. Nevertheless, there was a continuity of ideas between the two periods. Martí's words against the danger of US expansion struck a chord among radical nationalists like Castro who witnessed the contempt with which some Americans treated Cuba. In 1949, for example, Castro led a protest action against a group of drunken American sailors who had desecrated the statue of the

'Apostle' in Havana by urinating over it. Martí's call for Spanish America to declare its 'second independence', this time against the colossus of the North, also invoked an old tradition of Pan-Americanism without the United States derived from the epoch of the 'Liberator' of South America of the early nineteenth century, Simón Bolívar, to whom Castro was also deeply drawn,[10] This same vision can be found in Castro's restless search in the sixties to create a continent-wide revolutionary movement or more recently to form a united front with other Latin American countries around the issue of debt. Like Castro later, Martí believed that Cuba's struggle for independence was pivotal to the new balance of power in the American continent and beyond. 'We are holding a world in balance: it is not just two islands [Cuba and Puerto Rico] that we are going to free,' he wrote in 1894. 'An error over Cuba,' he said, referring to the danger of US invasion, 'is an error in America, an error among modern humanity.' Echoing Martí's words almost a century later, Castro remarked to foreign journalists in 1983 that 'North Americans don't understand . . . that our country is not just Cuba, our country is also humanity'.[11]

Martí's passionate belief in social justice, in the need for universal education, in the virtues of the countryside and land cultivation, found an echo in the young Castro. His conviction in the power of ideas and moral principles cannot fail to have influenced Castro, who gave special importance in his speeches and broadcasts in the fifties to explaining his purpose and who has rarely omitted in his speeches since the Revolution an appeal to rationality and ethics. Castro's language may be more prosaic but his faith in the capacity of ideas to move people to action was as great as Martí's when the latter wrote:

> Trenches of ideas are worth more than trenches of stone. There is no prow that can cut through a cloud of ideas.[12]

Underlying this confidence in the power of will was a historicism or belief in the intrinsically progressive nature of history derived in Martí's case from the philosopher Krause.

Both Martí and Castro also possessed an idealistic, almost ahistorical picture of a true Cuba, free from the aberration of dictatorship, whose essence was waiting to be discovered. Despite his espousal of Marxist-Leninist orthodoxy, Castro shared with Martí a vision of nationhood rather than class as the driving force of progress. In a passage highly reminiscent of Castro's words many years later, Martí wrote, with reference to the Latin American republics of the nineteenth century:

> The republics have purged in tyrannies their incapacity to understand the real elements of the country, derive from these the form of the government and govern with them. To govern in a new country is to create. . . . To know is to resolve. To know the country and govern it in accordance with this knowledge is the only way of delivering it from tyranny.[13]

This notion of *cubanidad*, an essential Cuban way of being from which the country had been alienated, was transmitted from one generation of radicals to another and re-interpreted in the light of their own political ideas. Those who had gained power in the new Republic, whether as politicians or businessmen, were considered to have squandered the inheritance of the independence struggle. Without exception, the Cuban governments since 1902 had been characterised by graft and corruption on a scale that seemed to grow with each new President. The almost undisguised practice of using public office for self-enrichment became a way of life. In part, it was a custom derived from colonial days when Spanish officials – civil servants, judges, policemen, and the like – were paid low salaries on the expectation that they would make up the rest through graft. It was also indirectly an expression of the dependent and subordinate status of the Cuban bourgeoisie. Hostage to the big neighbour across the Straits of Florida, whose entrepreneurs dominated so much of the island's economy, Cuba's rich men and rulers failed to project any set of universal values or mythology of nationhood of their own. Instead, their values were shaped by the culture of the United States; indeed, they tended to send their children to be educated in American universities, and many had second homes there. They were good at defending corporate interests

12

but failed to unite around the collective defence of their class interests.

Moreover Cuba lacked any powerful institution that might serve to bind together the different social classes. The old landed oligarchy had been swept aside by war and technological change. Economic interests were expressed through narrow corporate channels rather than political parties. The Church had been discredited to some extent by its close association with the Spanish elite on the island. Unlike most other Spanish American countries where Catholicism destroyed the indigenous Indian religions and served to integrate the poor into society, the Church failed to take root among the blacks of Cuba, among whom the African religious cult of *santería* was widespread. Without any unifying purpose to their hegemony, Cuba's rulers squabbled among themselves about the distribution of power and economic surplus, turning to their US godfather to settle disputes through armed intervention and a degrading form of paternalism, interim administration by American proconsuls. The belligerent US Senator Cabot Lodge wrote to Theodore Roosevelt in 1906:

> Disgust with the Cubans is very general ... the general feeling is that they ought to be taken by the scruff of the neck and shaken until they behave themselves. ... I should think that this ... would make the anti-imperialists think that some peoples were less capable of self-government than others.[14]

The political parties of the Republic had brought parliamentary democracy into disrepute by fraudulent electoral practices. So deep was political cynicism among Cubans that the feeling was widespread that they were incapable as a race of governing themselves. The patronising, racist image of Cuban incompetence shared by many Americans became absorbed into Cuban culture. The sentiment was expressed in the forties by the *choteo criollo*, a form of self-disparaging, cynical humour directed against the establishment.[15] The crisis of legitimacy in Cuba was exacerbated by the fragility of its governments faced with the fluctuations of sugar prices on the world market.

The twin blights of the Cuban Republic, its economic and cultural subordination to the United States and the corruption of its political life, were challenged by two successive student movements in the early and late twenties. These became for the new rebels among Castro's generation an almost mythical reference point. Both occurred at times of severe economic dislocation caused by a crash in sugar prices on the world market and were accompanied by considerable labour unrest. The first movement coalesced around demands for the reform of the corrupt university system in Cuba but moved on rapidly to embrace a more wide-reaching critique of society. Cuba's leaders were accused of having betrayed the independence struggles by delivering the island over to American interests or passively acquiescing in US hegemony, and by indulging in self-enrichment at the expense of the people. The student movement of 1923 was part of a continent-wide revolt in Latin America by middle-class youth against imperialism and military dictatorship and for radical reform and nationalist regeneration. Deeply influenced by a combination of left-wing European ideas – anarchism, anarcho-syndicalism, and Marxism – and indigenous movements such as the Mexican Revolution, the students were nevertheless moved also by the resentment of a new middle-class generation whose access to positions of influence was blocked by nepotism and political corruption. This same generational conflict would play an important part in later movements of youthful rebellion in the early thirties and early fifties.

The most outstanding leader of the 1923 generation of students was the dashing Julio Antonio Mella, who founded the Cuban Communist Party in 1925 with the old anarchist and close collaborator of Martí, Carlos Baliño. Mella's murder in 1929 by the dictator Machado's assassins while Mella was in exile in Mexico won him a place in the already lengthy roll-call of martyrs for Cuba's redemption. It also saved him from the disrepute suffered later by the Party he had co-founded, which collaborated with the authoritarian governments of the forties in obedience to the zigzag policies of the Third International. In the figure of Mella in particular, Marxism remained one strand of the tradition of nationalist redemption that the fifties' generation would take up again.

Castro's generation, however, was more directly and profoundly influenced by the Revolution of 1933 that had overthrown the dictator Gerardo Machado. That eventful year laid the basis for Castro's own revolution some fifteen years later. An ex-general and wealthy businessman, Machado had succeeded the corrupt President Zayas in 1925 on a reformist campaign promising the repeal of the Platt Amendment and an ambitious programme of public works. It soon became clear, however, that Machado was out not only to enrich himself but also to concentrate even greater power into his own hands. In 1927 (the year after Fidel Castro was born) he got the Congress, packed with suborned supporters, to approve a constitutional amendment prolonging his term of office from four to six years and giving him an additional two years' term without re-election. Machado further strengthened his grip over Cuban politics by creating an extensive patronage network and by violently repressing the emergent opposition among students and in the labour unions. Machado's state terrorism was answered by the rise of urban terrorist groups. Bombs were thrown, armed opponents of the government exchanged gunfire in the streets with the police, and prominent labour and student leaders were tortured or gunned down by Machado's henchmen.

Like their predecessors, the student rebels were impelled in part by frustration. The National University had been traditionally an important route to power and influence in society. But the widespread nepotism of Machado's government blocked the path of many an aspiring politician, aggravating the problems caused by the absence of career opportunities for graduates of the highly traditional university system in Cuba. The student rebels' manifestos were filled with anger at the corruption and authoritarianism of the Machado regime. Except for the demand for the restoration of democracy, however, the opposition to Machado, among students and other groups, was divided over objectives. These divisions, although shaped by the ideological preoccupations of the thirties, were carried over in different forms into the next decade when Castro began his university career. The majority faction of the student movement called for an end to Cuba's dependency on the US and a programme of social reforms. The left wing of the student movement, on the other hand, was led by Marxists and had a clearly anti-imperialist and anti-capitalist orientation. Another youthful organisation of the Left (later called Joven Cuba) led by the charismatic Antonio Guiteras, advocated a radical programme of reforms and a rather vague socialism. Unlike the Communists, who called for a united front among the anti-Machado forces, Guiteras believed that insurrectionary actions by small organised groups could lead the way to revolution. Among his first actions was the seizure of a small military barracks in the eastern province of Oriente; some twenty years later Castro was to attempt a similar action on a larger barracks in the capital of Oriente. For each group, the much-repeated slogan of the day, 'Revolution', meant a different thing; from the patriotic regeneration of Cuba to the seizure of power by the working class. Organised opposition to Machado was not confined to youth. Some middle-class professionals and bourgeois nationalists, recognising the need for political change (and anxious for more protectionist measures to safeguard Cuban industry) formed an underground terrorist organisation, the ABC, in an attempt to bring about Machado's fall by provoking US mediation.

Political unrest in Cuba in the early thirties was aggravated by the post-1929 world slump, which forced down the price of sugar and tobacco on the world market. Labour dissent against wage restraint and unemployment began among the sugar workers in 1933 and spread throughout the island. Armed groups of workers in provincial towns staged small insurrections. Disturbed by the state of virtual civil war prevailing in Cuba, the new US President Franklin D Roosevelt sent a special envoy to negotiate a transfer of power from Machado to a candidate more acceptable to the Opposition. The dictator, increasingly isolated among his own supporters, fled to the US one night in August 1933 and the presidential palace was sacked by the masses.

However, the new provisional government, put together with the help of Roosevelt's envoy and filled with respectable conservatives, hardly corresponded to the revolutionary atmosphere in the cities of Cuba. Machado's henchmen were being hunted down and lynched. The strikes continued. Sugar mills were seized by workers. Radical demands were spreading to new sections of society. Indeed, a new rebellion began in a totally unexpected quarter. Impelled by the fear of cuts and emboldened by the revolutionary turmoil, the army's NCOs staged a coup attempt that rapidly won the support of the students. Led by a sergeant stenographer of mixed mulatto and Indian origin, Fulgencio Batista, the revolt was couched in vague redemptionist terms that would appeal to a wide constituency of discontent. Batista proclaimed:

The revolution has not taken place merely for one man

to disappear from the political scene but for a change of regime, for the disappearance of the colonial system that 31 years after the 20th May 1902 has continued to drown the country.[16]

Attempts by conservative officers to mount a counter-coup failed and armed power rapidly came to lie in the hands of Batista, who elevated himself to the rank of colonel and chief of staff. Meanwhile, the students proclaimed a new five-man government headed by a professor, Ramón Grau San Martín, in which the popular Socialist Antonio Guiteras became Minister of the Interior. Unable to secure recognition by the United States and to quell the unrest in Cuba (Guiteras unsuccessfully calling on workers to return to work in order to help the new cabinet), the government of Grau fell after a hundred days.

The ex-sergeant Batista now held the future of Cuba in his hands, balancing for a short while the demands of students and workers against the interests of the anti-Machado but conservative sections of the bourgeoisie; indeed, Batista became the Bonaparte of the 1933 Revolution. From then on until 1959 he was to control political life in Cuba. Batista's rise to power had two broad explanations. Because of the institutional weakness of the different Cuban elites, the army was a relatively autonomous body and certainly the only organisation capable of imposing a political solution. Secondly, the officer class had been discredited to some extent by association with Machado while the NCOs, many of them from poor, rural, mulatto backgrounds, had been infected by the revolutionary atmosphere of the early thirties. Batista turned on those who continued to agitate for the radical reforms promised by the Grau government: strikes were put down with violence, and Guiteras was cornered in a house in Havana with a few supporters and shot dead after a long gun battle. Yet through the governments he effectively controlled in the second half of the thirties, Batista carried out a populist programme of reforms – limited land distribution, welfare schemes, paid holidays for workers, and the like – which took up some of the demands of the revolutionary movement of 1933.

For Castro's generation of rebels, however, the 1933 Revolution represented yet another failure, albeit the most heroic, to realise the historical aspirations of the Cuban nation stretching

17

back to the independence struggles of 1868. This sense of frustration was felt on a deeply personal level. Individual self-esteem and 'national dignity' became intertwined. The evidence of North American domination was all around. Cuban middle-class culture was permeated by its values and there was much in the behaviour of Americans, from their ambassadors to their sailors, to suggest the inferiority of the Cuban race. The servility and corruption of generations of political leaders, including many who had fought in the Wars of Independence, were seen as a betrayal. On the other hand, the revolutionary legacy of the past was a violent one. Because the political system in Cuba had so signally failed to fulfil its promises, attempts to bring about real change had been carried out through insurrection, armed action, and street riot. The student rebels, in particular, saw themselves as the true heirs of this nationalist tradition. They inherited from the past a conviction that it was their duty to carry on the unfulfilled struggle for independence and development on behalf of the true Cubans: the poor, the dispossessed, 'los humildes'. They also inherited a sense of their own power. It was the student movement that had led the fight to overthrow Machado and that had established the short-lived 'revolutionary' government of 1933. Despite the counter-revolution of Batista, students had forced the new government to recognise the inviolability of the university campus; the police were no longer allowed to enter its precincts.

When Castro enrolled in Havana University as a law student in 1945, the residue of the events of 1933–4 still dominated political life in Cuba. The action groups that had fought Machado still retained their guns even if they had lost their ideals. Some of the social and economic reforms that had been passed in the aftermath of the Revolution were enshrined in a new Constitution. Yet those who had profited by the upheaval had failed to honour its promises. While students were a privileged elite, from which traditionally the Cuban political class had drawn some of its leaders, their access to positions of influence through democratic channels and by virtue of merit continued to be blocked by the widespread use of patronage. The frustration felt by the new layer of students of the forties was deepened by the visible degeneration of the 1933 rebels into gang warfare and senseless vendettas. The

18

new generation of rebels came to see it as their mission to pick up the banner of national regeneration that had first been raised in 1868 and had been dropped by the wayside. The indigenous historical models that were available to them were neither peaceful nor particularly democratic. Any profound political or social change had come about through violence. The system of parliamentary democracy had proved not only unstable but incapable of delivering reform. It had also been a source of bottomless corruption. The heroes of Cuban history were dead heroes, almost by definition – young martyrs. Almost all the great men who survived the last War of Independence had become villains, seduced by power and wealth. The violence that brought about change arose from several sources: the insurrectionary strikes of workers, peasants and land labourers, the old and continuing tradition of rural banditry, and student power.

The historical legacy thus passed on to the new generation of politically inspired youth was made up of several radical strands that were woven together into a more or less coherent picture of the past and an almost millenarian vision of the future: the fight of the ex-slaves for complete emancipation; the international struggle against imperialism; the Utopian socialism and anarcho-syndicalism of Martí's working-class base; the liberal republicanism of Martí himself; the Communist movement of the twenties; the student rebellion of the thirties; the liberal nationalism of the middle class; and the unbroken struggle of Cuban workers in the town and the countryside for better wages and conditions. These different strands embodied contradictory aspirations, but they were bound together for the time being by the conviction that social and economic change was an indispensable component of national liberation. This radical heritage profoundly influenced the strategy of the young Castro in his rise to power.

. . .

NOTES AND REFERENCES

1. Thomas H 1971 *Cuba: the Pursuit of Freedom.* Harper & Row, New York, p. 1094
2. Azicri M 1988 *Cuba: Politics, Economics and Society.* Pinter, London, pp. 21–2

3. *Bohemia*, 6 and 20 March 1955, quoted in Winocur M 1979 *Las clases olvidadas en la revolución cubana*. Grijalbo, Barcelona, p. 45

4. From *Cuba Económica y Financiera*, May 1957, quoted in Winocur 1979, pp. 40–1

5. Letter to Manuel Mercado in Martí J J 1971 *Martí y la primera revolución cubana*. Biblioteca Fundamental del Hombre, p. 133

6. From Martí J J 1971 'Nuestra América', p. 17

7. Kapcia A, 'Cuban Populism and the Birth of the Myth of Martí, in Abel C and Torrents N 1986 *José Martí: Revolutionary Democrat*. Athlone Press, London, pp. 32–64

8. Conte Agüero L 1959 *Cartas del Presidio*. Lex, Havana, p. 60

9. Szulc T 1987 *Fidel: a Critical Portrait*. Hutchinson, London, p. 298

10. Franqui C 1983 *Family Portrait with Fidel*. Jonathan Cape, London, p. 9

11. Martí J J *Obras Completas*. Havana, vol 3, pp. 142–3; Castro F 1983 *Conversaciones con periodistas norteamericanos y franceses*. Politica, np

12. From 'Nuestra América', in Martí 1971, p. 11

13. From 'Nuestra América', Martí 1971, pp. 13–14

14. Quoted in Thomas 1971, p. 481

15. Solaun M 1969 'El fracaso de la democracia en Cuba', *Aportes*, July, pp. 72–3

16. Batista F 'Proclama al pueblo de Cuba', *Pensamiento Crítico*, April 1970, p. 217

Chapter 2

THE REBEL

There was little in Castro's family background to suggest he would become a rebel. His father was a self-made man who had emigrated from Spain towards the end of the last century, after having participated in the last independence war as a conscript in the Spanish army. Moving to the Mayarí region in Oriente, the easternmost province of Cuba, he had started his working life as a labourer laying the tracks for the railway of the local employers, the American United Fruit Company. Shortly afterwards, he had become a pedlar, selling lemonade to the plantation workers and then a variety of goods to local families. Like many Spanish immigrants, he was a hard worker and a determined saver, and with his savings, he had leased land from the United Fruit Company and begun to plant sugar cane to sell to the American-owned mills. By dint of hard work and careful accounting, he had become a wealthy planter.

For all their affluence, Fidel's family did not share the culture of the landowning class. His mother had been a maid and cook in the Castro household during his father's first marriage. Indeed, Fidel's parents may only have been married after the birth of his two elder siblings and himself in 1926. By all accounts Castro senior retained his rough and hard-working ways and brought up his children with a firm hand. There had been no traditional landed oligarchy in the area; the Mayarí region in which the family estate lay had begun to be exploited only in the late nineteenth century by American companies. Fidel Castro thus grew up amongst children of different social backgrounds. In his own rare accounts of his childhood, Castro likes to suggest that this early experience of socialisation among children of poor families was a formative influence on his political development.[1] It may have provided him with a certain social ease, yet he could not have helped feeling different, if only because his father owned most of the land and employed most of the workers in the immediate locality. Although he was not brought up with the traditional values of the landowning elite, Fidel did not belong either to the sophisticated urban culture of many of his future student companions. He was not a man of the people but nor was he a typical product of the upper or middle classes. How far this cultural indefinition played a part in Castro's formation is impossible to judge, but it must have influenced his own sense of being exceptional. Many years later, Castro said,

> I was born to be a politician, to be a revolutionary. When I was eighteen, I was, politically speaking, illiterate. Since I didn't come from a family of politicians or grow up in a political atmosphere, it would have been impossible for me to carry out a revolutionary role, or an important revolutionary apprenticeship, in a relatively brief time, had I not had a special calling.

Castro displayed rebelliousness towards authority from an early age, frequently getting his own way through a combination of persistence and boldness. When he was six or thereabouts, the young Fidel was sent to Santiago to lodge at his godparents' house while attending a local primary school in the city. Unhappy at the domestic austerity of his new home, he decided one day to break all the school's regulations in order to force his family to make him a boarder. This first successful act of rebellion was followed by other equally audacious exploits; the youthful Castro seems to have developed an early sense of his capacity to prevail over higher authority, to get round people and mobilise support, as he himself claimed in an interview many years after.[2] Later, he was educated in the strict, almost military atmosphere of Jesuit schools, first in the capital of Oriente, Santiago, and then in Havana. There, according to his own description, he learned values of self-discipline, enterprise, tenacity, and personal dignity that were the hallmark of Jesuit education.[3] The almost Spartan habits that he claims to have acquired during his schooling have not deserted him some fifty years later. At school, Castro stood out as a brilliant athlete and a popular

22

leader. In frequent excursions to the foothills of the Sierra Maestra near Santiago, he would go climbing and swimming and during his holidays would spend days exploring and hunting with a gun in the mountainous region around his father's estate, a practice that would stand him in good stead years later in his guerrilla war much deeper in the same Sierra Maestra.

Castro enrolled in the law faculty of Havana University in October 1945. He was then a tall, handsome nineteen-year-old brimming with vague ambitions and bold self-confidence. Photographs of the period reveal typically Spanish features; also a surprisingly boyish face and a rather formal, aloof bearing. He was soon embroiled in student politics; it was difficult to avoid them. Since the twenties, Havana University had been one of the centres of political life. Cuba's political elite traditionally had drawn many of its members from graduates of the university, in particular from the law faculty. In a society where class interests and political parties were imperfectly integrated, the highly politicised student movement was an important source of support or opposition. Recent events, moreover, had given the student movement a new prominence. To understand the political stage on which Castro made his first bow, we need to look briefly at the development of post-1934 politics in Cuba.

Since he shot to power during the 1933 Revolution, the ex-sergeant stenographer Fulgencio Batista had dominated political life on the island. Batista never entirely forgot his origins as a man of the people, a 'humble' mulatto who had risen to the rank of non-commissioned officer in an army led by a white, upper-class elite. Although he had turned on the anti-Machado movement in 1934, establishing a new government more acceptable to the United States and the Cuban establishment, he began to advocate a programme of social and political reforms that was hardly to the liking of his new allies. Through puppet cabinets, Batista carried out a series of measures designed to bring the sugar and tobacco industries under closer control of the state and to cushion the small growers and mill owners from the effects of fluctuating world prices. He also pushed through a number of reforms, such as a limited land redistribution, social benefits for workers, and a reorganisation of the tax system. The reformist drift of his policies was enshrined in the Constitution of 1940, a social democratic charter whose fulfilment became a major demand of the anti-Batista movement that Castro was to lead in the fifties.

Conscious of the growing opposition of the business and professional elites in Cuba, Batista sought for support among the popular masses, using his humble origins and natural charm to good effect. He also struck a deal with the Communists, legalising their party and allowing them to assume control of the reorganised labour confederation, the CTC. The Communists, following the new popular front policy of the Comintern in 1935, welcomed Batista as a 'democratic and progressive ruler' and were rewarded with two cabinet posts in his post-1940 government.[4] Shortly after, they renamed the party the Partido Socialista Popular (PSP), signalling their increasing drift away from internationalism and towards social democratic nationalism. Because the conservatives were divided, the main focus of opposition to Batista were the followers of the wealthy physician and university professor Ramón San Grau, the president of the short-lived revolutionary government of 1933–4. In exile for a brief period in the United States, Grau had organised his middle-class supporters into a new party, the Partido Revolucionario Cubano Auténtico, or Auténticos for short, indicating that they considered themselves the true heirs of Martí. In the elections of 1940, Batista, backed by considerable sums of money from newly won-over sections of the Cuban establishment and with the support of the Communists, won a majority of votes against the Auténtico coalition, which stood for the radical reformism of the 1933–4 government. Having for six years controlled political life from the wings, the ex-sergeant now became President of Cuba.

Apart from the army, now led by officers closely associated with his own fortunes, the new President had no organised base; nor did he represent ostensibly any one elite or social class in Cuba. In order to balance the different forces in Cuban society, with himself as the fulcrum, Batista followed an elaborate system of regulation and distribution that resembled in many respects a modern corporate state. The most powerful sectors of the economy – American and Cuban sugar growers and mill owners, cattle barons, tobacco farmers, industrialists, and organised labour led by the Communists – bargained through the ministries for the protection of their monopolistic privileges, sharing out among themselves the income generated by sugar exports, or the losses when world prices fell. Batista also set out to buy political support by using the proceeds of the national lottery; union leaders, journalists, churchmen, and the like received illegal pay-offs. State funds were also used to subsidise ailing companies and to stem unemployment. Batista's mix of corporatism and populist nationalism was part of a widespread trend throughout Latin America in the wake of the Depression of the thirties. In Argentina in the early forties, for example, Juan Domingo Perón set out on a similar path in an attempt to integrate capital and labour around a project of nationalist regeneration.

The World War years were a bonanza for the Cuban economy, the demand for sugar and minerals from the Allies drawing in considerable profits. Having amassed a fortune in real estate, Batista stood down in 1944, as he was required by the Constitution. His chosen successor was the prime minister, through whom he would have continued to exercise power had he won. In fact, the opposition coalition, led by the Auténticos, secured a slender majority against Batista's allies (who included the Communists). Grau San Martín was duly proclaimed President, bearing with him the hopes of many Cubans for social reform and honest government. Far from carrying out the promises of the 1933–4 movement, however, the Grau government inaugurated a new period of corruption exceeding that of Batista's presidency.

The Auténticos were an electoral party whose leaders were drawn almost exclusively from the professional middle class. Without any organised base and confronted with potential opposition from the army and the Communist-controlled labour unions, they used their control of the state coffers to maintain a patronage system whose main clients were the armed action groups left over from the anti-Machado struggle. One of the first actions of the Grau government was to hand out public appointments, such as city chief of police and state director of sports, to leaders of the different factions to reward them for their backing during the electoral campaign and to ensure their support in the future. His Minister of Education reputedly allocated $80,000 for their maintenance.[5] The political gangs, in turn, provided Auténtico politicians with a small private army to act as bodyguard and control over key police forces with which to counterbalance the power of the army. They also helped to intimidate opponents of government bosses and, where intimidation failed, they murdered. The streets of Havana came to resemble Chicago at the height of prohibition and the dailies were filled with gruesome photographs of victims. The degeneration of political life under Grau was exemplified by the prolonged gun battle on 15 September 1947 in the streets of Marianao, a satellite town of Havana, between two different police forces led by rival gangs.

The armed groups retained from the anti-Machado days a vague redemptionist rhetoric of social justice and honest government.[6] Their leaders were mainly ex-students who had played an important role in the revolutionary period of the early thirties. Drawn from a marginal social group without the ability to mobilise, they derived from that experience a belief in insurrection rather than class struggle as the path to power. There were few models in Cuban history suggesting that a constitutional parliamentary road to power could be successful. Despite their opposition to the United States, they were also fervent anti-Communists (though several had been members of the Party in the thirties) partly because of the collaboration of the Cuban Communists with Batista; the onset of the Cold War in 1947 deepened this hostility. The presence in their ranks of several relatively young veterans of the Spanish Republican army brought into their already bitter quarrels the divisions and resentments of the Civil War in Spain. Among the groups there was also a strong macho cult of physical heroism.

However, what divided the political gangs was not so much ideology as competition for political influence and public funds. The structure of power in Cuba, dominated by an informal corporatist system, offered few opportunities for self-advancement through legitimate democratic channels. The easiest route to political power lay through patronage. Auténtico bosses were ready to grant privileges to pay for the services of the armed groups or to buy off their potential opposition. In order to raise additional funds beyond government pay-offs, the gangs turned to extortion rackets as well. In a country with a high rate of graduate unemployment, graft and extortion became a way of life for dozens of middle-class youths. Having encouraged the armed groups from the outset, the Auténticos found themselves unable to control them. Gang rivalry became so intense that Grau's successor, Prío, arranged a truce between the groups in 1949, offering over 2,000 sinecures in the government as a price of peace.[7]

When Castro entered Havana University, student politics were permeated by the rivalry between two groups, the Movimiento Socialista Revolucionario (MSR) and the Unión Insurreccional Revolucionaria (UIR). The Communist-led student movement of the thirties had been displaced by a strong-arm group financed by the Auténticos and this in turn had been driven out by the MSR, which now controlled the student union. Both organisations held important positions outside the university (the MSR, for example, was awarded the post of chief of the secret police by Grau) but extended their organisation into the campus because domination of the student movement was a source of political power in itself. Situated on a hill in the middle of Havana, the campus was constitutionally a no-go area for both the police and the army. It was possible therefore to store weapons in its precincts; on several occasions gunfire was exchanged in its halls and squares and on the immense flight of steps leading up to the entrance of the university. The student electoral system was dominated by whichever group happened to be paramount physically, and in turn this organisation controlled life in the university, handling the sale of textbooks, for example, and even of stolen exam papers.

It was difficult for a politically ambitious student like Castro not to become caught up in one faction or another, and indeed, he had a brief association with the UIR during which he may have been involved in a number of violent actions. Many years later, he gave the armed factions the following epitaph:

> Those young people were not to blame. Driven by natural longings and by the legend of a heroic epoch, they wanted to carry out a revolution that had not been fulfilled at a time when it could not be made. Many of those that died as gangsters, the victims of an illusion, would today be heroes.[8]

In view of his own political activity in the university, however, it seems a somewhat generous judgement. Castro soon distinguished himself on the campus as a talented organiser and orator rather than a man of violence, though he was not lacking in youthful bravado. His initial preoccupation with student politics gave way during his second year to a broader concern with national problems. Unlike many of the activists in the university, however, Castro had had no political grounding. Neither his provincial upbringing nor his privileged education had helped him to define any clear political philosophy. Instead, he seems to have been concerned from the outset of his career with the problem of achieving power in the service of a rather vague ideal of nationalist regeneration. The earliest political contacts he made in the university reveal a pragmatism that would become a feature of his subsequent political career; among his new friends were the university leader of the MSR and president of the Students' Union, and a leading student member of Juventud Socialista, the Communist Party's youth organisation. What they shared was the same anger of their generation at the betrayal of Cuba's nationalist ideals by its politicians, an anger that transcended student factionalism. Castro's earliest speeches as a student representative were an attack against false leaders and government corruption. In one of the first of his speeches to be mentioned in the press, he declaimed, speaking to a meeting of student representatives in July 1947, 'Let us not be borne down by the pessimism and disillusion spread over the last few years by false leaders, those merchants of the blood of the martyrs.'[9]

Castro's rise to prominence as a student activist was fraught with mortal risk. He was openly criticising the Grau government as well as the MSR, which was closely associated with prominent Auténtico politicians. Increasingly he drew the fire of the MSR. Towards the end of his first year, he was issued a warning to keep off the campus by one of the most powerful police chiefs in Havana, a client of the Auténticos and a prominent member of the MSR. 'This was a moment of great decision,' he recalled later.

> . . . Alone on the beach, facing the sea, I examined the situation. To return to the University would mean personal danger, physical risk . . . an extraordinary temerity. But not to return would be to give in to threats, to admit defeat . . ., to abandon my own ideals and aspirations. I decided to return and I returned . . . with arms in my hands.[10]

He was later to say that the years he spent in the university had been more dangerous than the guerrilla war in the Sierra.

In the spring of 1947, Castro found the opportunity to channel his energies into a new political organisation outside the university. As a youthful critic of the Grau government, he was invited to join a new party, the Partido del Pueblo Cubano, called the Ortodoxos to indicate their fidelity to the ideals of Martí. Founded by an ex-student leader of the 1933–4 Revolution and leading Auténtico politician, Eddy Chibás, the Ortodoxos were a breakaway from the government party, mainly of its youth organisation and most of its membership in the traditionally radical province of Oriente. Chibás was a passionate and somewhat unstable man, prone to rhetorical flourishes and duels of honour like many Cuban politicians of the time (not excluding Castro himself). A radio journalist, he had been lambasting the Grau administration for its venality in regular broadcasts since 1945. Chibás' brand of patriotic and populist radicalism exercised a deep influence on the young Castro for whom no other models were available among the politicians of the day. Castro was drawn to Chibás' fearless style of moral denunciation as well as the new party's vague social reformism and anti-imperialism.

However, there was a notable difference between the two in their ostensible attitude to the Communists, providing an early indication of Castro's pragmatic approach towards political ideology. As the Cold War intensified in the late forties, Chibás became a fervent anti-Communist, reserving his bitterest criticism not for the United States but for 'a much greater danger: the threat that the totalitarian communist imperialism of Moscow, the most despotic, cruel and aggressive in History will spread across the whole world to destroy for many centuries the democratic form of government, the free will of nations, and the liberty of expression.'[11] Apart from an occasional protestation that he was not a Communist, Castro never indulged in Cold War rhetoric and was careful to avoid undue criticism of the Popular Socialist Party, the renamed Communist Party of Cuba. This was not because at this stage he secretly sympathised with their aims but because he was already concerned with uniting the opposition to the government. Contrary to some accounts that suggest that he was drawing ever closer to Marxist-Leninist ideas, Castro, in so far as he could be said to have a defined political philosophy, was a radical nationalist with strong beliefs about social justice.[12] In any case, the PSP hardly provided the sort of political model which Castro found for a while in the Ortodoxo Party. After collaborating with the Batista government in the early forties, the PSP had sought to make a pact with Grau in 1945 using its influence in the labour unions to gain political leverage. The new generation of young radicals, whose spokesman Castro was increasingly becoming, spurned the politics of both the Centre and the traditional Left of the Cuban party system. For Castro, then and in the future, tactical considerations were more important than ideology.

Within the new Ortodoxo Party, Castro soon became a leading exponent of a more radical strategy for political change. Gathering together a number of young members of the Party, including some who had been in the UIR gang, he formed a faction called the Acción Radical Ortodoxo. The new group sought to challenge the traditional electoral policies of Chibás and his followers and proposed a revolutionary road to power largely derived from the insurrectionary models of Cuban history. Several events between 1947 and 1948 encouraged Castro's natural inclination towards extra-parliamentary action. In the summer of 1947, he took part in an armed expedition to overthrow the Trujillo dictatorship in the nearby Dominican Republic. When the force had already gathered and had been trained on a deserted island off the eastern coast of Cuba, the expedition was aborted at the last moment by Grau, probably under pressure from the US government. On his return, Castro and some followers organised a brilliant public relations stunt by taking to Havana the bell of Demajagua, which had been rung in 1868 to launch the first War of Independence, with the aim of using it as a symbolic focus of an anti-government rally. In the rally and in subsequent demonstrations, Castro's ability to organise actions and to rouse the crowd with his impassioned oratory was already evident.

Another experience that influenced the young Castro towards an extra-parliamentary strategy was his fortuitous participation in the urban riots of April 1948 in Bogotá. In trouble with the police over a false accusation that he had been involved in the murder of an MSR leader and national sports director, he had managed to get himself on to the Cuban delegation to a congress of Latin American students in the Colombian capital. The congress, coinciding with the ninth

Inter-American Conference, had been sponsored by Perón, whose main aim was to win support for his claims on the Falkland/Malvinas islands by organising an anti-imperialist front among student organisations. The Cuban delegation, led by the rising star of the opposition, the young Communist Alfredo Guevara, was determined to deflect the main resolution towards condemnation of American rather than European imperialism.[13] During the conference, the leader of the Colombian Liberal party, Jorge Eliecer Gaitán, was assassinated on the same day that he was due to meet the Cuban delegation for a second time. Gaitán was the immensely popular leader of the Opposition, not unlike Eddy Chibás in his populist radicalism, and a politician whom Castro had admired from a distance. His murder occurred at a moment of great social unrest in Colombia and unleashed a popular uprising. In the frenzied atmosphere that followed, Castro joined with the crowds, according to his own account, having obtained a rifle and some ammunition and a policeman's uniform. Later he became involved with a large nucleus of forces led by rebel policemen. After forty-eight sleepless and risk-filled hours, Castro made his way to the Cuban Embassy and from there, together with the rest of the Cuban delegation, he was flown back to Cuba.

Many years later, Castro said of his experience in Bogotá: 'The spectacle of an absolutely spontaneous popular revolution has to have exercised a great influence on me.'[14] He had witnessed at first hand the intense energies that could be released by a single event catalysing the discontent of wide sections of the population. But without any central direction to channel these energies the uprising had been uncoordinated, and the opportunities that arose for seizing power had been lost. It must have strengthened in him the belief, sanctioned by Cuban history in part, that powerful movements of popular protest could emerge spontaneously but that a tightly knit group of professional revolutionaries was also necessary to organise them. The Colombian masses, he said later, 'failed to gain power because they were betrayed by false leaders'.[15]

Castro's experience over the next four years, between 1948 and 1952, further undermined any remaining belief he held that constitutional methods could lead to political and social change. Shortly after the Bogotá riots, Grau was succeeded as President by another Auténtico politician, Carlos Prío Socarrás, who became embroiled, like his predecessor, in the politics of corruption and patronage. At this time Castro, now twenty-two, married a young philosophy student from a wealthy Oriente family, Mirta Díaz-Balart, the sister of a university friend of his. Although they had a son a year later, Castro seems to have devoted little time to his new family, his life being consumed in political activities within and outside the university. In 1949, he finally managed to shrug off the long-standing and politically damaging accusation that he was a member of the UIR by boldly denouncing the secret pact recently made between the President and the gangs whereby the latter agreed to cease their feuds in exchange for government sinecures. Castro's public denunciation earned him widespread publicity but also the wrath of the gangs, and he was forced to go into hiding and then into voluntary exile in the United States for several months until the situation cooled down.

Returning later to Cuba, Castro devoted himself to his legal studies and graduated in 1950. With two other graduates, he set up a practice on a shoestring budget in a run-down district of Havana. For the next three years they took up the defence of victimised workers, slum-dwellers, detained students, and poor clients in general, hardly raising enough money to pay for the rent of the office. Castro wasted little time also in pushing his way into the public arena. A frequent guest on radio programmes and a regular contributor to the daily newspaper *Alerta*, Castro followed the example of his mentor, the Ortodoxo senator and journalist Eddy Chibás, in berating fearlessly the Prío administration for its corruption. The campaign of denunciation against the government, however, received a setback when, in a dramatic gesture, Chibás shot and killed himself at the end of a radio broadcast, having failed to produce evidence he had previously promised implicating the Minister of Education in acts of corruption. Chibás' suicide was the act of an unstable person but it also expressed the frustration of those who were trying to bring about change in Cuba through legitimate channels. Though Castro claimed for many years subsequently that his political programme was inspired by Chibás, he had clearly moved on to an altogether more radical strategy for change, as was evident from the internal debates among the Ortodoxos between the party

leaders and his own small faction, ARO. Castro learned a
lot from Chibás about public relations, in particular the
value of bold, emotive political broadcasting, but he was
not as convinced as Chibás was that moral campaigns were
enough.

For all his growing doubts about parliamentary action,
Castro threw himself into the elections of 1952. Having
been left off the Ortodoxo slate by a timid party leadership,
Castro got himself nominated as a Congressional candidate
by two poor districts. In the run-up to the elections, he
conducted a vigorous campaign, sending out thousands
of leaflets and delivering several speeches every day. The
Ortodoxos would probably have won the elections. Castro
claimed later that had he become a Congressman he would
have used parliament as a 'point of departure from which
I might establish a revolutionary platform and influence
the masses in its favour. . . . I was convinced then that it
could only be realised by revolutionary means and not as a
way of fulfilling these changes directly.'[16] In the meantime,
however, Batista, who had spent the intervening years in his
home in Florida without ever losing touch with Cuban politics,
returned to the island to lead a new military coup. Fearing an
Ortodoxo victory, he seized power before the elections could
be held and proclaimed himself chief of state. The dismal
experience of the governments claiming allegiance to the
1933 Revolution was thus brought to an end by the very
man who had launched the Revolution in the first place.

Batista's military coup of 10 March 1952 destroyed any
lingering idea Castro may have entertained that Cuba could
be regenerated through parliament. The existing political
system was too fragile to be the vehicle of radical reform.
The endemic corruption that for decades had characterised
Cuban governments was the result not just of personal greed
but of the weakness of political representation in Cuba. In
the absence of any institution embodying the interests of
the different elites, the parties in power sought to maintain
office by concession, patronage, and pay-offs. The result was
governmental paralysis. A reformist government, moreover,
would run the risk of intervention by the only effective political
force, the army, which was used to controlling the political
destiny of the island. Any movement to redeem Cuba would
have to confront the problem of armed power.

In any case, Castro was not inclined towards the rituals of parliamentary activity. Like many of his peers, his political ideas were inspired by the heroic and violent myths of Cuba's past. He had spent his university years organising protest actions, declaiming on the steps of the campus, and dodging batons and bullets. Indeed, he grew into manhood in a culture prizing oratory and physical heroism above all. Through political models such as Chibás, Gaitán, Perón, and even Mussolini, he was aware of the power of populist leadership, and he had experienced the extraordinary energy of the masses in revolt.[17] He had been drawn to the Ortodoxo programme of nationalist redemption and social justice but not to its parliamentary strategy. None of this suggests that Castro even considered himself a socialist. Some orthodox accounts, including his own, argue that he was moving rapidly towards Marxist ideas but can only adduce the fact that he was reading parts of *Das Kapital* and that he was harbouring extra-parliamentary strategies.[18] The core of Marxist strategy is the class struggle, and there is little evidence at this stage that Castro saw the activity of the Cuban workers as more than one element in his strategy for the seizure of power. It is true that among Castro's closest acquaintances were two Communists. Yet one has the impression from his writings, speeches, and actions in this period that he was relatively unsophisticated ideologically, drawing inspiration from many different sources, of which the most important were Cuba's nationalist traditions. Castro also appears as a political outsider, an upstart to some, drawing grudging admiration as well as exasperation from both the Ortodoxo leadership and the Communists. A restless, ambitious, immensely self-confident young man, with a sharp eye for political opportunities, he was also moved by vague ideals of progress and justice. The Batista coup, closing any path of self-advancement for middle-class youth and renewing a depressing tradition of authoritarian rule, presented the young Castro with a personal challenge from which it was not in his character to shrink.

. . .

NOTES AND REFERENCES

1. Betto F 1987 *Fidel and Religion*. Weidenfeld & Nicolson, London, pp. 127–8

2. Franqui C 1980 *Diary of the Cuban Revolution*. Viking Press, New York, pp. 1–8

3. Betto 1987 p. 114–22; Franqui 1980 p. 8

4. Dominguez J I 1978 *Cuba: Order and Revolution*. Harvard University, Cambridge, MA, p. 555, n 87

5. Suchlicki J 1969 *University Students and Revolution in Cuba 1920–1968*. University of Miami, p. 49

6. *Bohemia*, 15 June 1947, pp. 52–5

7. Thomas H 1971 *Cuba: the Pursuit of Freedom*. Harper & Row, New York, pp. 763–4

8. Llerena M 1978 *The Unsuspected Revolution*. Ithaca, New York, Cornell University Press, pp. 42–3

9. *Diario de la Marina*, 17 July 1947; see also *El Mundo*, 28 November 1946

10. *América Libre* 22–28 May 1961

11. From a radio broadcast on 1 January 1951 quoted in Conte Agüero L 1955 *Eduardo Chibás, el Adalid de Cuba*. Jus, Mexico p. 718

12. Castro later defined his position as 'Utopian socialist' while Lionel Martin and orthodox Cuban historiography see an early affinity on Castro's part to Marxist ideas.

13. Author's conversation with Tomás Gutiérrez Alea, 29 Aug. 1988

14. Szulc T 1987 *Fidel: a Critical Portrait*. Hutchinson, London, p. 123. For Castro's account of the Bogotazo, see pp. 120–3 and Franqui 1980 pp. 13–19

15. *América Libre*, 22–28 May 1961

16. Castro's statement is quoted in Mencía M 1986 *Tiempos Precursores*, Editorial de Ciencias Sociales, Havana, pp. 77–8

17. One of Castro's friends at the time and later a bitter opponent claims that among his favourite reading were the complete writings and speeches of Mussolini: Pardo Llada J 1988 *Fidel e el 'Che'*. Plaza y Janes, Barcelona, p. 30

18. Castro himself in evidence to Frei Betto 1987 pp. 141–3; Martin L 1978 *The Early Fidel*. Lyle Stuart, Secaucus, New Jersey, pp. 60–4

Chapter 3

RISE TO POWER

Batista attempted to present his coup of March 1952 as a progressive action designed to bring an end to corruption and anarchy in Cuba. To this effect, he promised to carry out a number of social reforms and eventually to hold elections; he had not lost his populist touch. The promises could not have been more cynical, for he began his new rule by suspending constitutional guarantees such as the right to strike, and abolishing both Congress and political parties. Yet the political system of Cuba had been so discredited by eight years of Auténtico administration that many Cubans welcomed his coup. The Cuban business establishement and the small conservative parties rallied to his side while the executive of the Cuban Labour Federation, the CTC, whose left-wing leadership had been destroyed by repression in the late forties, made a deal with Batista in which they agreed to collaborate in exchange for corporatist favours.[1]

The most resolute opposition to the coup came from the student movement, which staged demonstrations throughout the island. By contrast, the top Auténtico politicians chose to flee to the US whilst the Ortodoxo leadership dithered over what response it should make to the abolition of their party, finally issuing a call for a very tame campaign of civic resistance. It took over a year for the two organisations, now in exile, to agree to a joint statement demanding the restoration of democracy, the Ortodoxo rank and file being divided over whether to enter into any pact with the Auténticos. A more serious split that led to punch-ups between members separated those who advocated peaceful resistance and others, led by Castro, who were campaigning for more violent methods. The timidity of the Ortodoxo leadership increasingly exasperated the younger activists. With his usual boundless energy, Castro was already organising a clandestine network and an underground press, and by the autumn of 1952 he was calling for a different leadership based on a new generation of activists. In his mimeographed paper, *El Acusador*, he wrote,

> The present moment is revolutionary, not political. Politics is the consecration of the opportunism of those who have means and resources. The Revolution opens the way for true merit, for those who bare their chest and take up the standard. A Revolutionary Party needs a young revolutionary leadership drawn from the people in whose hands Cuba can be saved.[2]

By mid-1953, he had organised about 1,200 followers, mostly from the Ortodoxo youth, into 150 cells, based mainly in the westernmost provinces of Havana and Pinar del Río.

Castro was not the only conspirator. In a repeat of the Machado years, several middle-class underground organisations were set up; one of these, the Movimiento Nacional Revolucionario, tried unsuccessfully to carry out a coup within the army in April 1953 with the aid of some officers who were members of its underground network. By that time, Castro had drawn up his own very different plans for armed action. Inspired by several famous incidents in Cuban history, he and his co-conspirators planned to seize a military barracks in Santiago, the capital of Oriente province, calling on the people of Cuba to rise against the new dictator. The plan was rash but not as foolhardy as it might appear. Oriente was by tradition a rebellious province. It was from here that the movements of independence had been launched against the Spanish colonialists occupying mainly the western provinces; the spark that had set alight the rebellions had been the seizure of barracks and the distribution of their weapons. The east–west divide in Cuba is fundamental to an understanding of its history. For centuries, the easternmost province had been largely isolated from the rest of the island by mountain ranges and ocean currents. While the western provinces had been settled by immigrants, the east became Cuba's frontier land where escaped slaves and fugitives from the law found refuge. In the late nineteenth century, Oriente had been at once the poorest and most Cuban of the island's provinces and the most rebellious against the rule of Spain. It had also been the scene of numerous slave revolts, and more recently of sugar workers' uprisings. In the early thirties, urban guerrilla groups led by Antonio Guiteras had carried out several actions against the Machado dictatorship. In the fifties, it was the east that suffered the highest level of unemployment on the island; Oriente accounted for almost 30 per cent of the jobless. Living standards were also considerably lower there than in the west and political dissatisfaction, consequently, was higher.

The geographical position of Oriente also offered a strategic advantage; it could be cut off from the rest of the island if the only road from the west could be blocked. Militarily, the plan was relatively simple if fraught with risks. The rebels were to seize the Moncada barracks and distribute arms to the people. A separate armed group would capture the barracks at Bayamo, some 100 kilometres away, holding up the deployment of reinforcements on the road from the west. If the uprising were to fail, the rebels would retreat into the densely wooded mountains of the Sierra Maestra, there to begin a rural guerrilla campaign.

The weakness of the plan rested on the faith that the people of Oriente would rise up spontaneously in response to the exemplary action of Castro's band. The rebels had no organisation in Santiago itself; in fact, only one of their number came from the Oriente capital and there was only one cell in the whole of the province.[3] Some measure of the *naïveté* of the scheme is afforded by the broadcast that the plotters hoped to put out once the barracks had been seized. Written by a young poet under the supervision of Castro and in the name of 'The Cuban Revolution', the proclamation laid claim to the traditions of Cuba's independence struggles in the year of Martí's centenary. It also called for the moral regeneration of society, promising economic development and social justice, without explaining the means whereby these were to be achieved. The manifesto was to be followed by an appeal for a national uprising, a recording of Chibás' farewell speech, and heroic music, including Beethoven's Eroica and Chopin's A flat Polonaise.

In the event, the action failed because of a chance encounter near the gates of the barracks with a military patrol. Dressed in military uniform, Castro and his men were fired on and forced to retreat before they could penetrate into the barracks square. Two other groups of rebels were positioned behind the building to give covering fire. One, led by Castro's brother, Raúl, had occupied the roof of a nearby block, and another, led by the joint leader of the action, Abel Santamaría, had seized a hospital building at the back of the barracks. The latter group, not knowing of the failure of the assault, remained in the hospital where they were captured by soldiers and shot in cold blood or tortured to death. The two women taking part in the action witnessed the beatings inflicted on some of the prisoners; one of them, Abel Santamaría's sister Haydée, was brought her brother's gouged-out eye by a sergeant. Fleeing by car, Castro and some of the survivors made their way into the nearby Sierra to hide from the patrols that soon began to scour the hills behind Santiago.

In Bayamo, the smaller group of rebels had had as little luck, failing to reach anywhere near the barracks before they were fired on and forced to abandon the assault. During the next few days, the fleeing rebels were picked up in groups or individually by the army and the rural guard. Many were summarily shot; of the 111 men who had taken part in the action, sixty-nine died, only eight of them killed in combat. Castro himself, with a small band of survivors, was finally captured after six rough days of flight in the mountains. Unlike many of their comrades, their lives were saved thanks to the resolute action of the black lieutenant commanding the detachment that discovered them; concerned to avoid their cold-blooded murder, he insisted on delivering them to the city gaol rather than the Moncada barracks where an irate garrison awaited them. Other rebels were saved by the intervention of the Archbishop of Santiago at the head of a group of civic leaders. The Archbishop himself drove into the mountains and prevented further shooting. Finally, the arrested rebels were taken to the large gaol on the outskirts of the city to await trial.

The attempted capture of the Moncada barracks on 26 July 1953 has been presented in some orthodox accounts as the first stage in a more or less defined strategy leading to the proclamation in 1961 of a Marxist-Leninist

39

state.[4] What evidence we have of Castro's thinking at the time suggests, on the contrary, that the object of the assault was to spark off a popular revolt leading to the restoration of democracy, the installation of an Ortodoxo provisional government, and the celebration of general elections.[5] Nevertheless, the government programme of social reforms and nationalisations that Castro had in mind was not one which could have been acceptable to the Cuban bourgeoisie nor to the United States. It was likely therefore that he had already moved beyond a social democratic policy of radical reform within the existing political framework and envisaged an eventual clash with the established order.

None of this proves, however, that Castro was inspired by Marxist ideas or Leninist strategy, as he later claimed.[6] The action and the programme of Moncada were firmly within the Cuban tradition of radical nationalism, whose main representatives were Martí and Antonio Guiteras; more so, indeed, than another hero of Cuban history, Julio Antonio Mella, who was more closely associated, as a young Communist of the twenties generation, with working-class internationalism. The plan to seize the barracks derived from Cuban history, not from the Russian Revolution (though Castro and Abel Santamaría were reading Lenin's *State and Revolution* at the time). It was also the desperate gesture of a marginal social group with few links with organised workers. To claim, as some commentators have done, that the Moncada action had a proletarian character on the basis of the occupations of the assailants is to indulge in tokenism.[7] While most of them had a working-class background, only one or two were from the organised labour movement; indeed, the majority were workers in marginal or casual occupations such as delivery men, building workers, waiters, street vendors, cooks, and the like, while several were self-employed or unemployed. The vast majority were rank-and-file members of the Ortodoxo party whose founder had been a visceral anti-Communist. The 26th July Movement, as it soon came to be called, had popular roots, unlike all the other anti-Batista underground groups except the Communists, but it was not a working-class organisation.

In the trial that followed in September, Castro proclaimed the programme for Cuba's regeneration which the rebels had been unable to broadcast. Castro conducted his own defence and he later reconstructed from memory his long and brilliant speech to the court, using the notes taken by a follower during the trial; the speech was to become later the official testament of the Cuban Revolution. Standing before the judges in a borrowed toga, Castro launched into a wide-ranging critique of the political, economic, and social situation in Cuba. At pains to establish a legal justification of the Moncada assault, he linked the action with the revolutionary traditions of Cuba, quoting Martí repeatedly, and invoked universal principles such as the right of rebellion against despotism derived from many centuries of history. The names of Dante, John of Salisbury, St Thomas Aquinas, Knox, Milton, Thomas Paine, and others rang out in the tiny sweltering room of a small tropical town, and it must have bewildered the few people allowed to be present. Castro ended his long speech on a defiant note:

> I know that prison will be hard, harder than it has been for anyone, filled with threats, with callous and cruel barbarity, but I do not fear it, just as I do not fear the fury of the despicable tyrant that tore out the lives of seventy of my brothers. Condemn me, it does not matter, history will absolve me.[8]

Castro's defence speech took the form of a manifesto to the people, *el pueblo*, from whom he deliberately excluded 'the well-off and conservative sections of the nation'. Although he was careful to keep within the framework of the 1940 Constitution, in reality Castro was proposing the complete transformation of Cuba from a semi-developed, dependent society into a modern, progressive nation. The speech contained the blueprint of most of the social and economic reforms that the new regime would attempt to carry out after the victory of the Revolution in 1959. Many years later, Castro characterised the Moncada programme thus: 'whoever reads it carefully and analyses it in depth will see, in the first place that it was a programme of national liberation, a very advanced programme and a programme that was very close to socialism'.[9] Because of its radical nature, orthodox accounts have portrayed the speech as a Marxist document, arguing on one hand that Castro had to conceal the full extent of his revolutionary plans because the moment was not ripe and on the other that he was reinterpreting Marxist-Leninist thought to suit the special nature of the Cuban situation.

They are right to point out the continuity of Castro's programme for reform. But it was not exclusively a socialist programme. In the same year of the Moncada assault, the reformist government of Colonel Jacobo Arbenz was carrying out the first stages of a similar programme in an attempt to transform the semi-feudal economy of Guatemala into a modern capitalist one. Moreover, what is missing from the Moncada manifesto and 'History will absolve me' speech is the central notion of Marxism: the self-emancipation of the working class. Castro's programme of 1953 belonged to a different tradition, that of anti-colonial, nationalist regeneration, in which radical reform and nationalisation were, in theory at least, compatible with a modified capitalism. This is not to deny the influence of Marxist ideas on Castro's thinking. But in 1953, he was a Martí follower, *tendance* Marx, not the other way round.[10]

The Moncada action and the trial brought Castro vividly into the public eye. In a nation used to violent gestures of rebellion, the assault on the barracks evoked widespread admiration while the much-publicized brutality of the army awakened the sympathies of many Cubans for the survivors. When Castro began his fifteen-year sentence on the Isle of Pines, off the western coast of Cuba, he was already something of a national figure. A year after the assault, he was paid a courtesy call in gaol by the Interior Minister and two other cabinet ministers in a tacit recognition of his new status. The nineteen months he and twenty-five of his comrades spent on the island before they were amnestied were devoted to study and discussion. There the foundations of the 26th July Movement were laid, and a new strategy for the seizure of power forged. Although he had no reason to believe he would be amnestied, Castro's optimism seemed boundless. It did not seem to desert him even when he was put into solitary confinement for organising the chanting of the 26th July hymn within earshot of Batista, who was paying an official visit to the island.

Only once did he seem to lose heart. In July 1954, he learned that his wife, Mirta Díaz-Balart, whose brother was Vice-minister of the Interior in Batista's cabinet, had been accused of being on the payroll of the Ministry. The much-publicized news was deeply hurtful to Castro on both a political and personal level. Always able to deal effectively with political attacks, he seemed to crumble for a short while before what he perceived as an assault on his honour. In a surprising transposition of a typically Castilian code of aggrieved sexual honour on to a political plane, he wrote disbelievingly to a friend: 'The prestige of my wife and my honour as a revolutionary is at stake. Do not hesitate to return the offence, and wound back to an infinite degree. Let them see me dead a thousand times rather than suffer impotently such an offence!' The accusation also brought out Castro's latent prejudice against gays, a strong component of Cuban machismo at the time. Attacking the Interior Minister for his claim, he wrote, 'Only an effeminate like Hermida who has sunk to the last rung of sexual degeneration could stoop to such a procedure, marked by such indecency and lack of manliness.' When it became clear that the accusation was true, Castro issued divorce proceedings against his wife. On the edge of despair, he wrote to a close friend and political collaborator: 'I consider the 26th July [Movement] far more important than my own person and the moment I know that I cannot be useful to the cause for which I have suffered so much, I will take my life without hesitation, all the more so now that I have not even a private ideal left to serve.'[11]

Meanwhile, the campaign for the freeing of the Moncada prisoners had gathered widespread support and found a sympathetic echo in the press. In May 1955, Batista, anxious to appear benevolent, signed an amnesty bill and Castro and his comrades were released unconditionally. To considerable acclaim, the young rebel returned to the political fray, launching renewed attacks on the regime. Batista was facing an upsurge of protest against his rule and responded by tightening his measures of repression. The opportunities for agitation were narrowing every day and increasingly Castro feared he might be re-arrested or even assassinated, a fate that had befallen many other opponents of the dictator. His brother Raúl sought asylum in Mexico, and Castro himself, after taking farewell of his young son Fidelito, left Cuba for Mexico barely six weeks after his release, there to prepare for a fresh attempt to overthrow the dictator.

The new strategy was an extension of the original plans for the Moncada assault. Castro would land with a force of men on the west coast of Oriente where they would be met by around a hundred combatants of the 26th July Movement and several lorries. The combined force would seize the nearby town of Niquero and then move up the coast to capture Manzanillo. The landing would coincide with uprisings and strikes in Santiago and Guantánamo. A campaign of agitation and sabotage would follow, leading, it was hoped, to a general strike that would topple Batista.[12] Unlike Moncada, the new plans did not rely on a single exemplary action that might spark off a spontaneous uprising. Another lesson had been learnt from the 1953 fiasco: beyond the armed groups there had to be a grass-roots organisation to provide arms, recruits, and logistic support, and to agitate among workers and civic groups for the crucial general strike. As in the Moncada plan, however, the rebels would move into the Sierra Madre to begin a rural guerrilla campaign should the original endeavour fail.

Castro had left behind in Cuba the bare bones of the new 26th July Movement. His followers on the island set to work to build the organisation from scratch. In most of the historical accounts of the Revolution, their efforts have received little attention; indeed, the Sierra campaign that began in 1957 has unjustifiably overshadowed the labour of the 26th July militants in the towns and the countryside. Their main recruiting ground was the Ortodoxo branches throughout the island, but especially in Oriente where the Movement began to lay popular roots. There was considerable support among Ortodoxo militants for Castro's strategy of armed resistance in contrast to the leadership's policy of political agitation. At a congress of Party members in August 1955, Castro's message calling for a 'revolutionary line' received a standing ovation and chants of 'Revolution'; at provincial party assemblies the same response was heard.[13] By early 1956, Castro felt sufficiently strong to break publicly with the Ortodoxo leadership and declare the new Movement.

The 26th July militants' work of agitation and recruitment was divided into geographical and functional sectors. In the western tip of Oriente (now called the province of Granma)

44

where the landing of Castro's force was planned, there were separate groups of industrial workers, agricultural labourers, peasants, fishermen, and students. The largest town near the projected landing place, Manzanillo, had a long tradition of labour protest among its sugar workers, dockers, shoemakers, and tobacco workers. In the local union elections of 1956, militants sympathetic to the Movement came close to gaining control of the union branches but were forced to withdraw because of threats by the military.[14] Many workers drawn to the 26th July Movement were young Ortodoxo supporters impatient with the Party leadership. The Communist rank and file organisation, the *Comités pro Defensa de las Demandas Obreras* was avoided by many sections of workers because of the PSP's previous collaboration with Batista; indeed there was a strong anti-Communist sentiment among many Cuban workers.

This explains in part the care Castro took in building bridges with the anti-Batista opposition. Although he would shortly be in contact with the Communists through two top-level emissaries who visited him separately in Mexico in 1956, Castro roundly denied any links with the PSP. In gaol for several weeks in Mexico City after a police round-up, the result probably of pressure from the Cuban authorities, Castro had an article published in the weekly Cuban paper *Bohemia*, rejecting a claim by Batista in the previous issue that he was a Communist. 'Of course,' he wrote, 'the accusation of being a Communist seemed absurd to all those in Cuba who know my public career, which has been without any kind of links with the Communist Party.' In a barely disguised attack on the PSP's previous collaboration with Batista, Castro went on,

> What right, on the other hand, does Batista have to speak about Communism when he was presidential candidate of the Communist Party in the 1940 elections, when his electoral posters appeared under the hammer and sickle, when he was photographed alongside Blas Roca and Lázaro Peña [two top Cuban Communists], and when half a dozen of his present ministers and close collaborators were leading members of the Communist Party?[15]

Castro's denial was clearly meant to reassure many of his followers in Cuba who opposed the Communists. But it also marked his distance from the PSP, which was calling for a non-violent, united-front policy of opposition to the dictatorship. While he may have been drawn to certain Marxist ideas at this stage, Castro had no illusions about the Cuban Communist Party.

He took care also to spread wide his net of contacts. The planned expedition needed considerable sums of money. Besides the flow of cash from the Movement in Cuba, several large contributions were made by wealthy sympathisers; not least among them was ex-President Prío, now in exile in Miami. Like Martí some sixty years previously, Castro went on a fund-raising tour of the Cuban communities in Florida and along the East coast of the United States, giving rousing speeches to enthusiastic audiences and raising large sums of money. In August, Castro reached an agreement with the *Directorio Revolucionario*, a student-based, armed, underground organisation, led by the president of the Students' Union, José Antonio Echeverría, to operate jointly in armed actions in preparation for the forthcoming invasion.

By October 1956, the expeditionary force had been assembled and trained. Their instructor, Alberto Bayo, was an expert in guerrilla warfare, a veteran of the Spanish military campaign against Moorish guerrillas in the twenties and a Loyalist general during the Spanish civil war. A measure of Castro's powers of persuasion was that Bayo gave up his job and sold his business shortly after meeting him in order to train the would-be Cuban invaders in what must have appeared a madcap project. He wrote later that Castro 'subjugated me. I became intoxicated with his enthusiasm. . . . Then and there I promised Fidel to resign from my . . . [job] and to sell my business.'[16]

Among the expeditionaries was a young Argentinian doctor, Ernesto Guevara, soon nicknamed 'Che' by his new companions. Guevara had abandoned his career as a doctor in Argentina in 1953 to work for the radical reformist government of Guatemala. He had helped in abortive attempts to resist the invasion of a CIA-trained army which overthrew the Arbenz government in 1954. Angered by the role of the United States in Latin America and deeply moved by the terrible poverty he had witnessed in his travels throughout the continent, Guevara became convinced of the need for armed revolution. After the Guatemala experience, he had moved to Mexico and plunged himself into the works of Marx and Lenin. A man with a strong will and a clear mind, he took immediately to Castro and joined the expedition less than twelve hours after meeting him for the first time. In contrast to the more parochial concerns of the Cuban revolutionaries, Guevara brought to the leadership of the expedition a vision of a wider Pan-American struggle against US imperialism.

Disregarding the advice of both the Communists and the leader of the 26th July Movement in Oriente, Frank País, Castro decided to set sail before the end of 1956. The Communists were opposed to the idea of the invasion in itself. In a letter a few months later to the American journalist Herbert L Matthews, the PSP President wrote, 'In these days and with reference to assaults on barracks and expeditions from abroad – taking place without relying on popular support – our position is very clear; we are against these methods.' What Cuba needed, he went on, was 'democratic elections'.[17] The Communists argued that if the expedition had to take place it should at least wait for the beginning of the cane harvest in January when it might coincide with strike activity. Less than twelve months previously, a quarter of a million sugar workers had come out on strike after their wages had fallen by 23 per cent following a cut in Cuba's sugar quota on the world market and the decision by the United States to increase its own production. The strike had taken on insurrectionary proportions in some places; workers had seized town halls and clashed with the army.

For his part, the young 26th July leader Frank País had insisted that the organisation in Oriente, the stronghold of the Movement, was not ready for the invasion.[18] But Castro would brook no delay. He had promised publicly that he would return to Cuba before 1958. Any postponement, moreover, might jeopardise the expedition that was now ready to set sail; the Mexican police had already been alerted to the activities of the Cuban oppositionists. Castro's decision to go ahead with the expedition illustrated once again his belief in the overriding importance of public relations and his faith in the triumph of will over logistics.

Logistically, indeed, the invasion turned out to be a disaster. Setting sail on 25 November on a yacht which was intended to carry less than half the load, the eighty-two-man expedition ran into a storm, had mechanical breakdowns, was forced

47

to jettison supplies, lost its way, and landed at the wrong place on the wrong day. Two days before the yacht Granma beached in a muddy estuary on 2 December, Frank País' armed group had attempted to stage an uprising in Santiago, but after some thirty hours of sporadic gunfire against the police and the army they had been forced to abandon the enterprise. Forty-eight hours later, wading painfully through a mangrove swamp, the ragged and exhausted invaders finally landed on dry ground. Castro announced grandly to the first peasant they came across, 'I am Fidel Castro and we have come to liberate Cuba.' Four days later, another peasant betrayed them to the Rural Guard, who were searching the area for the expeditionaries. In the devastating ambush that followed, Castro's expedition was all but destroyed. Of the eighty-two men who had set out, only sixteen (though legend conveniently has it that there were twelve) remained alive or free to start the war against the modern army of the Batista regime. ╱

Some of the anecdotes of that terrible episode tell of Castro's apparently absurd optimism. After being dispersed in the ambush for several days, a demoralised Guevara with a handful of unarmed men managed to reach the main group high up in the Sierra Maestra. Seeing them arrive, Castro exclaimed, excitedly pacing up and down on a hilltop overlooking a valley, 'Batista's fucking had it now!'[19] What saved the expedition, however, was not Castro's confidence, although that must have helped to raise morale, but the peasants of the Sierra Maestra.

The agrarian structure of the rough and isolated Sierra was very different from that of other parts of Cuba's countryside. Most of the peasants were squatters who made a precarious living off small parcels of land belonging to local *latifundistas*. A continuous war was waged by the landlords' foremen to prevent them encroaching any further on their territory. According to the colonel in charge of the operation to destroy Castro's expedition, 'From these struggles there arose constant fights between the squatters and the foremen and their followers, with the result that sometimes a foreman or one of his men died and at other times it was a squatter who was killed or who had his hut burnt down.'[20] Several generations of peasants had fought attempts by the army or the Rural Guard to evict them; some were regarded by the authorities as nothing better than bandits. The mobility of these peasants, and their intimate knowledge of the people and the terrain of the Sierra enabled Castro's band to survive and begin to grow in number. The army's brutal treatment of peasants suspected of sheltering the rebels helped to provide the first recruits of the new guerrilla force, although many were frightened into evacuating the area at the beginning.[21] Furthermore, Castro's policy of paying for the food purchased from the peasants, of executing their most notorious persecutors, and putting his men to work in the coffee harvest in the spring of 1957 turned their initial sympathy into active support. As Castro's unit became established and moved into new areas, it absorbed small bands of poorly armed fugitives and bandits who had fled to the remotest regions, there to fight the occasional skirmish with the rural guard. The guerrilla struggle in the Sierra had existed long before the arrival of Castro and his fighters.

It had not been Castro's intention to wage the war almost entirely from a rural base, nor were the peasants of the Sierra Maestra typical of the Cuban countryside as a whole. Yet as the campaign against Batista gradually centred on the Sierra, a new mythology arose about peasant rebellion and rural virtue that was to underpin the future legitimacy of the Revolution and influence the Left world-wide. In this new version of rural populism reminiscent of the thinking of the Narodniks and the Chinese Communists and articulated above all by Che Guevara, the city was seen as a source of corruption while a somewhat idealised peasantry replaced the urban proletariat as the revolutionary class of Cuba. The war in the Sierra could not be described in any sense as a peasant war. The guerrilla leaders were city people, although they took on the emblematic guise of the land, and many of the rank and file were volunteers recruited in the towns by the 26th July Movement. The urban underground was heavily engaged in sabotage, agitation and logistical work in support of the military campaign in the mountains; during the struggle against Batista, according to one calculation, it carried out over 30,000 acts of sabotage. Yet, as one ex-guerrilla later wrote, having abandoned Cuba after it became aligned with Moscow, 'The Comandante and his Twelve Followers were the revolution, not the city, the clandestine war, the 26th July Movement, the strikes, the sabotage, the people's boycott of Batista's elections. The revolution was the hero not the people.'22

The two-year campaign that led finally to the defeat of the Batista regime marked the gradual shift away from the original plan to combine sabotage, guerrilla activity, and urban agitation to a strategy of full-scale engagement with the regular army. The ability of the rebels to repel military units not only eroded the morale of the rank-and-file soldiers but also strengthened the belief that the army could be defeated by military means. As the guerrilla forces consolidated their hold in the mountains, the centre of opposition to Batista increasingly became the liberated zone in the Sierra. This change of emphasis was accelerated by two things: the relative failure of anti-Batista actions in the city, and the skilful radio and press campaign carried out by Castro from his mountain fastness.

Other forces besides the 26th July Movement were attempting to topple the regime. In March 1957, the student-led underground organisation, the Directorio Revolucionario, made a wild bid to eliminate Batista at a stroke by attacking the National Palace. They were beaten back and many perished in the aftermath, including the popular student leader José Antonio Echevarría. In May, a guerrilla expedition financed by ex-President Prío landed on the north coast of Oriente but was betrayed by a peasant and wiped out. In September, some officers and sailors of the naval base at Cienfuegos staged a mutiny which was to have been part of an island-wide coup by anti-Batista elements in the armed forces. The isolated mutineers were easily crushed by forces loyal to the regime. These abortive actions only served to raise Castro's stature as the leading opponent of the dictator.

The point was underlined by the public relations campaign he conducted from the Sierra. Since his student days, Castro had learnt the value of using the media to drawn attention to his ideas. He had also become aware of the opportunities for agitation offered by radio broadcasting through his old mentor, Eddy Chibás. Barely ten weeks after the Granma landing, he staged a publicity stunt that did more for his standing than any military engagement. Under his instructions, M 26 organisers smuggled a willing *New York Times* journalist, Herbert L Matthews, into the depths of the Sierra to interview Castro, whom many had claimed to be dead. With a force of only eighteen men, Castro managed to give the impression, by careful stage management and some talented acting on the part of his followers, that he controlled a wide area of the mountains and had considerable numbers under his command. Published in the *New York Times* and later reported in the press in Cuba, where censorship had recently been lifted, Matthews' article caused a sensation, not least because it suggested that Castro's force was invincible.

Another important media coup was the installation of a radio station in the spring of 1958 by which time the rebel forces controlled a large area of the Sierra. Radio Rebelde brought a new dimension to the guerrilla war. Castro used its airwaves with great effect to put over his programme for reforms, and the regular news bulletins featured in the broadcasts gave a conscientiously accurate report of military engagements, in marked contrast to the triumphalist fantasies of the pro-Batista media. By the end of the campaign Radio Rebelde was vying with light music frequencies for popularity.[23]

A year after they had landed, Castro's forces dominated the Sierra Maestra. Below them, the army attempted to lay siege but the flow of messengers, arms, and recruits to and from the guerrilla stronghold and the city slipped through the army patrols without undue difficulty. Castro was joined by one of the Movement's most effective organisers in Oriente, Celia Sánchez, who became his companion and personal assistant from then on until her death in 1980. In the Sierra, the rebels had set up rudimentary hospitals, workshops for making light arms and ammunition and leather equipment, and a printing press in addition to the radio station. At this stage, the army, stung by a number of small defeats, chose not to make any military excursions into rebel territory, so that an uneasy truce reigned.

Divisions were emerging, however, between Castro and the leadership of the 26th July Movement on the rest of the island, the so-called *llano,* who now constituted a majority of its National Directorate. Castro's new strategy consisted in extending rural guerrilla warfare to other parts of the island, laying siege to the cities from the countryside; the general strike was the final blow that would topple Batista. Although urban sabotage and civic agitation still had an important role to play, the main function of the *llano,* in

51

Castro's view, was to service the guerrillas.[24] The Movement's leaders outside the Sierra, on the contrary, still clung to the strategy of the urban uprising and the general strike as the main instrument of Batista's overthrow. Castro repeatedly complained that they were holding back on arms, while the *llano* organisers, according to Guevara, showed signs of 'a certain opposition to the *caudillo* who was feared [to exist] in Fidel, and the militarist faction represented by us, the people in the Sierra'.[25] Although he showed complete faith in Castro, the brilliant 26th July organiser in Oriente, Frank País, was quite prepared to reorganise the movement, centralising its command into the hands of a few leaders and setting up new civic fronts, without consulting Castro.[26]

The idea that workers would spontaneously come out on strike against the regime was given a boost by events that followed the murder by the police of Frank País, in August 1957. Protest strikes spread from his home-town of Santiago to the provinces of Camagüey and Las Villas, forcing the government to suspend constitutional rights. It was a testimony of the close links that bound the Movement in Oriente to many sections of workers in the eastern part of the island. But workers in western Cuba, especially in the province of Havana where most of the labour force was concentrated, did not join the action. This was not surprising since País was hardly known there but it also highlighted the more radical traditions of the labour movement in the east of Cuba. Nevertheless, the experience of the August 1957 strikes, together with the optimistic reports coming in about the mood among workers, encouraged Castro to call for an island-wide general strike in the spring of 1958. In a speech on Radio Rebelde after the August strike, Castro had said, 'the spontaneous strike that followed the murder of our comrade Frank País did not overcome the tyranny but it did point the way towards the organised strike'.[27]

Most accounts of the strike of 9 April consider it to have been a total failure. It failed to dislodge Batista, and indeed, encouraged the dictator to believe for a short while that events were moving his way once again. According to the American Ambassador, 'Batista apparently felt he was in the ascendancy.'[28] Yet it did mobilise thousands of Cuban workers. In Las Villas province, most industries and services came to a halt; the town of Sagua La Grande to the north of the province was taken over by workers and held for a while against the army and the air force. Camagüey province was swept by strike action for two days, while the towns of Oriente were paralysed by strikes and street fighting. In the west, however, only a few thousand workers came out and there were only isolated acts of sabotage.[29] In fact, it was a repeat of the strike pattern of August 1957. But the lesson that was drawn this time was the opposite one.

In a crucial meeting of the Movement leadership in the Sierra twenty-four days later, the *llano* leaders were attacked for failing to organise the strike sufficiently, for relying on spontaneity and not involving workers in its preparation, indeed for the very assumptions that had underlain Castro's strategy for Moncada. The strike had been prepared in secret by the small network of Movement supporters among the workers, the National Workers' Front (FON), and depended on an appeal to workers over the radio to down tools. It seems also that the Movement's labour organisers refused to involve the Communists in the preparations, the organisers of the 26th July Movement sharing a long-standing distrust of them.[30] But a more important explanation for the relative failure of the strike, apart from the distinction between the labour movement in the East and West, lay in the fact that it did not occur at a moment of generalised labour protest, nor was it clear that Batista's regime was on the brink of collapse. Nevertheless, the conclusion drawn by the meeting was that it had not succeeded because of the shortcomings of the *llano* leadership and that, although the perspective of a general strike should be maintained, the main emphasis from then on would be on the military campaign.[31]

The action of 9 April was a watershed in the anti-Batista struggle. It strengthened Castro's leadership of the 26th July Movement, and discredited the *llano*'s organisers. The National Directorate was transferred to the Sierra and Castro became the supreme commander of the Movement. His faith in the labour and civic fronts in the towns was rudely shaken. In a bitter letter to Celia Sánchez he wrote:

> No one will ever be able to make me trust the organisation again. . . . I am the supposed leader of this Movement, and in the eyes of history I must take responsibility for the stupidity of others, and I am a shit who can decide on

nothing at all. With the excuse of opposing caudillism, each one attempts more and more to do what he feels like doing. I am not such a fool that I don't realise this, nor am I a man given to seeing visions and phantoms. I will not give up my critical spirit and intuition and especially, now, when I have more responsibilities than ever in my life.

I don't believe a schism is developing in the Movement, nor would it be helpful for the Revolution, but in the future, we ourselves will resolve our own problems.[32]

The event also marked the beginning of a *rapprochement* between the PSP and himself; without a trustworthy base among workers, Castro would need to cultivate allies in the one party that seemed to have some reliable grass-roots support. The PSP, conscious of Castro's growing stature, were also keen to establish closer contact and by September 1958 had a top-level member permanently in the Sierra. The failure of the 9 April general strike, finally, reinforced the moral hegemony of the rural guerrilla over the city. The campaigns in the urban centres of Cuba, whether they were sabotage, demonstrations, propaganda, or strike action, fatally weakened the Batista regime. The city may have its share of martyrs in the mythology of the Revolution, but it is the war in the mountains that furnishes the national epic of contemporary Cuba.

Indeed, the Sierra campaign was the mould that shaped the future Revolution. The rebel army came to be seen by Castro and his closest followers not only as the source of power in the new state but also as the instrument of social change. As the so-called liberated zones in the mountains were extended, the commanders began to carry out expropriations and enact laws that would be the basis of agrarian reform in the coming Revolution. The official morality of the future society, honouring self-sacrifice, solidarity, military discipline, and loyalty, was forged among the soldiers of the rebel army. The Sierra campaign provided the tightly knit group that would form the core of the Revolution's leadership; over thirty years later, Castro's closest confidants were veterans of the Granma expedition, whereas only one *llano* organiser held a position of any importance in the regime.

It seems likely, then, that the future course of the Revolution was delineated sometime between the consolidation of the guerrillas towards the end of 1957 and the summer of 1958, in the aftermath of the events of 9 April. In official accounts, Castro appears to have had it all worked out since Moncada. Those who broke with the new Revolution after its triumph, on the other hand, claim he changed course and betrayed its ideals. It was clear that he had a programme which could not be carried out in the framework of the traditional party system in Cuba. The betrayal thesis rests on a failure of imagination. Cuba could not undergo such radical changes without a transformation of its internal political system and even a re-alignment of its foreign relations. At the same time, it is difficult to believe that, before the consolidation of the rebel army, Castro had a clear picture of the direction that the future Revolution would take. He had a radical programme of reforms but not a well-defined political model. One has the sense that throughout the fifties he was feeling his way politically and strategically. In the Sierra, the path and the destination became more defined. In the rebel army he had built a concrete power base to carry out the structural changes he envisaged for Cuba. After the strike of 9 April he began to turn to the Communist Party as a source of organised support.

Above all, his political ideas became more clearly shaped under the influence of his two closest advisers, his brother Raúl Castro and Che Guevara. Both men were unorthodox Communists, the first because he had supported Fidel in what the PSP considered pure adventurism, and the second because he was impelled more by a Pan-American, anti-US nationalism than support for Moscow. But both were more familiar with Marxist ideas of whatever tendency than Castro. Guevara, moreover, had lived through the bitter experience of the destruction by the CIA of a government that had tried to carry out a programme of reforms similar to that planned by Castro. In the Sierra, they were the only rebels of any political sophistication and both had the opportunity to discuss the future course of the Revolution at length with Castro. Under their influence, the idea of a Cuban version of 'socialism in one country' may have begun to take shape in Castro's mind as a model for the future development of Cuba independent of the United States. There is no reason to doubt the painstakingly honest Guevara when he wrote in December 1957 to Frank País' successor in the 26th July Movement:

> Because of my ideological background, I belong to those who believe that the solution of the world's problems lies behind the so-called iron curtain, and I see this Movement as one of the many inspired by the bourgeoisie's desire to free themselves from the economic chains of imperialism. I always thought of Fidel as an authentic leader of the leftist bourgeoisie, although his image is enhanced by personal qualities of extraordinary brilliance that set him above his class.[33]

Whatever his political definition at the time, Castro was taking care to avoid raising suspicions among the anti-Batista opposition and in the United States that he wanted to go beyond the framework of a restored democratic system in Cuba. While Batista still remained in power, he needed the support of the opposition. But he was quick to denounce any rival claims to the leadership of the anti-Batista movement. In the autumn of 1957, the Movement's representatives in Miami signed an agreement with a new united front of the opposition, the Junta de Liberación Cubana, whereby Castro's forces would be incorporated into the regular armed forces once Batista had been overthrown. Learning of this unauthorised move that would have deprived him of his armed power base, Castro broke from the Junta. His rebel army was beginning to score victories against Batista's army while the organisations of the opposition had failed in their attempts to storm the Presidential Palace or to stage a mutiny in the armed forces. However, after the abortive April strike and the start of an all-out offensive by the army in May, Castro was forced to moderate his position. In July, he issued a manifesto known as the Caracas Pact, signed jointly with all opposition forces with the exception of the Commun-

ist Party. In it there was no mention of radical reform. Instead, the document referred to the restoration of constitutional and democratic rights and made a
vaguely worded promise of economic and social progress
that could have issued from the Auténticos themselves.

It was no coincidence that Castro's search for unity with
moderate and conservative opponents of Batista occurred
as the army launched a mass offensive against the guerrilla stronghold. Since the rebel forces had established
themselves in the Sierra Maestra, the army had made
several unsuccessful attempts to dislodge them. By March
1958 Castro had felt confident enough to establish new
fronts in Oriente. Raúl, for instance, had gone with a
column to the Sierra Cristal in the eastern part of the
province, where the rebels began to enact a wide-ranging
programme of social reform in the newly liberated zone.
The failure of the April 1958 strike, however, had encouraged Batista to believe he could rout the rebel army.
Twelve thousand troops, backed by the air force, had
been sent to destroy the rebel forces in both Sierras.

The failure of the offensive was the story not so much
of the military strength of the guerrillas as of the moral
weakness of the regular army. Already unpopular among
large sections of the population for their association with
the dictatorship, many officers and soldiers had little
stomach for fighting. Several units had gone over to
the rebels and there had been many desertions.[34] In
contrast, the guerrillas were a highly disciplined body.
An influential moderate supporter of the Movement later
recalled that during a visit to the rebel hideout the scene

> was like something out of the movies, watching them
> coming, taking positions all around, and all in complete
> silence. Everything there was said in whispers. I spent
> a month speaking in whispers: it was their discipline,
> the difference between the Rebel Army and the Batista
> army. The Batista army always arrived shouting, and it
> was easy to surprise them because it was known they
> were there.[35]

By September, Castro was ready to move the main force of guerrillas out of the Sierra Maestra and towards Santiago, the capital of Oriente. Shortly afterwards, he sent Guevara and Camilo Cienfuegos, a young worker from Havana and veteran of the Granma expedition, on an epic march to the centre of the island at the head of two separate columns. For these operations and for the final offensive, Castro needed money and political support. His new moderation was designed to attract the backing of wider sections of the population than those sympathetic to the 26th July Movement. And indeed, money began to flow in, no longer only from the civic and labour fronts of the Movement but now also from sugar-mill owners, sugar farmers, cattle ranchers, bankers, and industrialists, especially in Oriente.[36] What led increasing numbers of businessmen to support the rebels was not just the growing unpopularity of Batista but also Castro's call for national regeneration. Restricted by the US sugar quota and increasingly under pressure from North American sugar-beet producers, the Cuban sugar barons, for example, were responsive to appeals for a reform of Cuba's economic policy and political system. Castro's interviews for American journals between February and April 1958 were intended to reassure the business elite that they had nothing to fear from the Revolution and much to gain. Speaking in February to a journalist from *Look* magazine, who had been led by guides for four days and nights along mountain trails to the guerrilla headquarters, he declared,

I know revolution sounds like bitter medicine to many businessmen. But after the first shock, they will find it a boon – no more thieving tax collectors, no plundering army chieftains or bribe-hungry officials to bleed them white. Our revolution is as much a moral as a political one.[37]

Having beaten back the army, the rebel forces launched their own general offensive. Castro's column from the West and his brother's from the East advanced into the heart of Oriente, capturing town after town until they surrounded Santiago. Guevara's and Cienfuegos's units cut the island in half, preventing the flow of reinforcements from the West and then moved on Havana. With his army rapidly disintegrating, Batista made preparations to leave Cuba. Meanwhile, a group of senior army officers were plotting to replace him with a mixed civilian and military junta, which, they were assured, would be recognised by the US government. On New Year's Eve Batista fled to the Dominican Republic. The junta that replaced him enjoyed only a brief moment of power. From his headquarters just outside Santiago, Castro issued a call for a general strike to overthrow the military coup that was answered by the vast mass of workers. By the evening of 1 January, the junta had collapsed. The next day, Castro entered Santiago in triumph and shortly afterwards, to widespread jubilation, Guevara and Cienfuegos took control of Havana.

Batista's regime fell above all because it was barbarous. Thousands of his opponents had been tortured or murdered or both. But it also fell, just as it had risen to power in 1934 and 1952, because it did not represent any social class. Even the military was sharply divided, as the Cienfuegos naval mutiny had shown. Batista's closest advisers were officers who had risen from the ranks with him in the 1933 Revolution. Their power and privilege were resented by the more professional officer elite drawn from Cuba's middle class, among whom conspiracies had multiplied. The tacit consensus among sections of the population that had underpinned Batista's regime at first had crumbled because he proved unable to deal with any of the problems that concerned them. Corruption was still rampant, the poor were still as poor. Batista's support among the organised working class had withered. Unemployment in 1958 had risen from 8.9% in January to 18% in December. Only the top layer of the union bureaucracy still identified with the regime because it had nowhere else to go. Batista had lost his populist base, but he had not endeared himself either to the indigenous elites that controlled much of Cuba's wealth. His coup in 1952 had not brought violence to an end, as many Cubans had hoped, but, on the contrary, had engendered yet more. To the instability of the Cuban political system was added a growing sense of material insecurity among the middle class. Although they enjoyed one of the highest living standards in Latin America, their income had suffered a decline in the fifties owing to rising inflation and a steady fall in the price of sugar on the international market. *Per capita* income in Cuba had fallen by 18% in the two years following the coup and by 1958 had dropped to its 1947 level. Between 1956 and

1957, meanwhile, the prices of basic foodstuffs had risen by up to 40%.[38] A new economic downturn in the second half of 1958 created a generalised discontent while the tightening of economic competition and control from the United States encouraged sections of the middle class and the bourgeoisie to look favourably on the assertive nationalist policy promised by Castro. Like the rebel army itself, the climate of unrest spread from the East of the island, where traditions of rebellion were stronger, until it engulfed the West.

Batista's regime failed also because it was illegitimate. He had seized power on the eve of general elections that favoured another candidate and had maintained his rule through repression; the two presidential elections of 1954 and 1958 were fraudulent exercises in democracy. But his dictatorship had not been thorough because he was too preoccupied with the search for an elusive consensus of the kind he had enjoyed in the forties. While curbing the freedom of the press, he had also allowed it to criticise his regime when he had felt more secure. Castro managed to get no less than twenty-five denunciations of Batista published in Cuban periodicals. Indeed, the dictator had underestimated his most determined opponent, setting him free after he had served less than two years of a fifteen-year sentence, and minimising the threat posed by the rebel forces until it was too late. His army, without any effective counter-insurgency aid from the United States, conducted a campaign notable for its brutality and bungling; when the United States belatedly declared an arms embargo it was more of a psychological than a material blow.

Of the traditional political forces in Cuba, the military had been the only one that commanded any national authority. The elites that owned the island's wealth had proved incapable of uniting around a national project. The conservative parties had been too fragmented to be a focus of representation, while the Auténticos were discredited, having consistently reneged on their promises to end corruption. The only party with any substantial electoral support had been the Ortodoxos, but they lacked a well-defined ideology as well as an organisation and, besides, their popular leader was dead. The failure of the political system was due to a great extent to the contradictions engendered by Cuba's uneven and dependent development. A relatively well-developed society, Cuba could not carry through any much-needed and desired structural reforms while it was trapped by its sugar monoculture. Any attempt to do so threatened to incur the displeasure of the United States, whose military or merely diplomatic interventions had largely determined the course of Cuban politics in the past.

Castro thus stepped into a power vacuum that was not entirely of his making. He had skilfully seized the opportunities offered by a conjunction of historical conditions that were unique to Cuba. His success, moreover, owed as much to his imaginative use of the mass media as to the guerrilla campaign. Through the radio and the newspapers, he had attracted widespread admiration for his courage and patriotism. Indeed the rebel leaders of the Movement were moved by a high-minded and selfless sense of historical mission that seized the imagination of many Cubans, starved of heroic models among the politicians of the day.[39] By 1959 Castro had become the repository of many disparate hopes for Cuba's regeneration. As he had made his slow triumphal way by road from Santiago to Havana, he was treated as the last in the long line of Cuban heroes – the last, because, unlike the others, he had survived and prevailed.

. . .

NOTES AND REFERENCES

1. Mencía M 1986 *El Grito de Moncada*. Política, Havana, vol 1, pp. 110–14
2. *El Acusador* no. 3, 16 Aug. 1952, quoted in Mencía M 1986, p. 250
3. Mencía M 1986 *Tiempos Precursores*. Editorial de Ciencias Sociales, Havana, p. 123
4. E.g., in Fernández Ríos O 1988 *Formación y desarrollo del estado socialista en Cuba*. Ciencias Sociales, Havana; and Mencía *El Grito* 1986.
5. Castro's letter to Conte Agüero on 12 Dec. 1953 in Conte Agüero L 1959 *Cartas del Presidio*. Lex, Havana, p. 21
6. Castro's speech to the Caroline University of Prague in Ministerio de Educación Superior 1983 *La Revolución Cubana* 1953–1980, vol 1 pp. 245–9; see also in the same book, Mirta Aguirre's article 'El Leninismo en la Historia me absolverá', pp. 251–79

7. E.g., Martin L 1978 *The Early Fidel; Roots of Castro's Communism.* Lyle Stuart, Seacaucus, NJ, p. 116
8. Ministerio de Educación Superior 1983 p. 244
9. Castro F 1977 *Fidel Castro habla con Barbara Walters.* Carlos Valencia, Colombia, p. 30
10. Cf. Martin 1978, p. 122
11. Letters to Luis Conte Agüero, 17 and 31 July 1954, in Conte Agüero 1959 pp. 46 and 52
12. Faustino Pérez in *Bohemia,* 11 Jan. 1959 p. 38; also 'Los Sucesos del 30 de Noviembre de 1956', in *Bohemia,* 6 Dec. 1959, pp. 48–51 and 121–3
13. Castro F 'El Movimiento 26 de Julio', in *Bohemia,* 1 April 1956
14. Testimony of Celia Sánchez in Museo de la Clandestinidad, Santiago
15. *Bohemia,* 15 July 1956, pp. 63 and 84–5
16. Szulc T 1987 *Fidel: a Critical Portrait.* Hutchinson, London, pp. 250–1
17. Matthews H L 1961 *The Cuban Story.* Braziller, New York, pp. 51–2
18. Mencía 1986 *Tiempos Precursores.* pp. 309–10
19. In the original, 'Ahora sí, Batista se jodió'; as Guevara recounted: author's conversation with Tomás Gutiérrez Alea, 29 Aug. 1988
20. Colonel Pedro A. Barrera Pérez, quoted in García Montés J and Alonso Avila A 1970 *Historia del Partido Comunista de Cuba.* Universal, Miami, pp. 553–4 n. 5
21. Guevara E 'Un año de lucha armada', *Verde Olivo,* 5 Jan. 1964
22. Franqui C 1980 *Diary of the Cuban Revolution.* Viking Press, New York, p. 509; and 1983 *Family Portrait with Fidel.* Jonathan Cape, London, p. 35
23. Castro F 1973 *Fidel en Radio Rebelde.* Gente Nueva, Havana
24. See, e.g., Castro's letter to Celia Sánchez on 11 Aug. 1957 in Franqui 1980, pp. 220–1
25. Quoted in Szulc 1987, p. 350
26. País' letter to Castro, 7 July 1957, in Franqui 1980, pp. 202–5
27. Winocur M 1979 *Las clases olvidadas en la revolución Cubana.* Grijalbo, Barcelona, p. 100

28. Smith Earl E T 1962 *The Fourth Floor*. Random House, New York, p. 128
29. Details from *Carta Semanal*, 23 April 1958, quoted in *Hoy*, 9 April 1964
30. See 'Una reunión decisiva', in Guevara E 1968 *Obra Revolucionaria*. 2nd edn, Era, Mexico, p. 237; and in 1970 *Obras* 1957–67 (2 vols), Maspéro, Paris, vol 2 p. 98
31. *Hoy*, 9 April 1964
32. Letter to Celia Sánchez, 16 April 1958, quoted in Franqui 1980, pp. 300–1
33. Franqui 1980, p. 269
34. Pérez L A Jr 1976 *Army Politics in Cuba 1898–1958*. University of Pittsburgh, pp. 153–5
35. Raúl Chibás to Tad Szulc in Szulc 1987, p. 333
36. Domínguez J I 1978 *Cuba: Order and Revolution*. Harvard University, Cambridge, MA, pp. 128–9
37. *Look*, 4 Feb. 1958
38. Pérez L A Jr, 1988 *Cuba. Between Reform and Revolution*. OUP, New York
39. See, e.g., the correspondence between Castro and Frank País and Celia Sánchez in Franqui 1980

Chapter 4

DEFYING THE EAGLE

'When I saw the rockets that they fired on Mario's house, I swore that the Americans are going to pay dearly for what they're doing. When this war is over, I'll start a much longer and bigger war of my own: the war I'm going to fight against them. I realize that will be my true destiny'.

Fidel Castro in a letter to Celia Sánchez, 5 June 1958, after US-supplied missiles had destroyed the house of a peasant supporter of the Castro movement.[1]

When Castro took power in January 1959, his objective was nothing less than the transformation of Cuba into a developed and independent nation. He intended to achieve this extraordinary feat by mobilising the island's internal resources, with or without the help of other states or even against their wishes. The main agency of the regeneration of society would be the disciplined and selfless elite purged by prison and battle that he led. The most influential leaders of the Revolution were middle-class professionals or intellectuals used to working with the machinery of the state. Their own position in society, added to the peculiar nature of the 1959 Revolution, encouraged the belief that the social and economic restructuring of Cuba could be accomplished from the commanding heights of a new centralised state. They shared the conviction with many of the post-colonial regimes ⁓n the Third World during the fifties that central planning ⁓s essential for development, ensuring, moreover, that the ⁓efits of economic growth were distributed equitably. The ⁓cal changes ensuing in Cuba flowed from above, even if ⁓ad the support of the overwhelming mass of its people.

The new regime had come about not through a social but a political revolution and its power derived from the military victory of the rebel army that had operated on the margins of society.

The obstacles that faced Castro and his closest followers were formidable. In order to carry out their plans for a sweeping transformation of the island they had to destroy the old order; they had to convince or neutralise their influential liberal allies; and they had to confront the economic interests, both domestic and foreign, that controlled Cuba's wealth. Above all, they had to face the inevitable wrath of the United States, whose administration was the same as that which had helped to destroy the reformist Arbenz regime in Guatemala less than six years previously. For all his overriding sense of self-confidence, Castro proceeded cautiously at first. Among the revolutionaries there were few with any political experience. The rebel army, semi-literate if disciplined, was hardly a source of administrative skills. The enthusiasm of the crowds needed to be organised if they were to defend the Revolution.

During the Sierra campaign Castro had been careful to create the widest possible consensus among the anti-Batista opposition; while he had made it clear he was seeking to transform society, he had also issued calls for a return to the traditional democratic order in Cuba based on parliamentary elections and respect for private enterprise. From his mountain stronghold, he had named as President of the post-Batista provisional government a widely respected judge sympathetic to the 26 July Movement, Manuel Urrutia Lleó. Upon Batista's fall, Urrutia nominated a cabinet drawn from moderate members of the Movement while Castro himself was confirmed as Commander-in-Chief of the new armed forces. It was a government acceptable to most sections of public opinion in Cuba and the United States.

It soon became no more than a token administration, however. In a characteristic move, Castro set up an unofficial committee of his closest advisers, including his brother Raúl and Che Guevara, and it was this Office of Revolutionary Plans and Co-ordination that in reality set the agenda of the Revolution in its early days.[2] At the same time, following earlier contacts during the war, Castro began discreet negotiations with leading members of the Communist Party, whi officially still regarded his Movement as a petty-bourgeois formation. He hoped thereby to fuse the Communists with the radical wing of the Movement, using the experience and the organised base of the PSP to help create the new institutions of the Revolution on his own terms. In May, the National Institute of Agrarian Reform (INRA) was set up, with Castro as its President, to administer the moderate Agrarian Reform Act, the centrepiece of legislation in the early days of the Revolution. During the months that followed, INRA became an unofficial parallel government staffed by Castro's closest advisers.

The pace of Castro's reforms was determined partly by how confident he felt that the resulting tensions could be controlled. From his first day in power in Havana he had shown how he could mobilise an irresistible force among the great masses who supported him. When the rival urban guerrilla organisation, the Directorio Revolucionario (DR), had shown a reluctance to give up their arms to the rebel army, he had turned the crowd against them and they had capitulated. His plans for reform were also helped by the lack of cohesion among the economic elites in Cuba. The Agrarian Reform Act, for example, which envisaged a modest expropriation of large landholdings excluding the most important sugar and rice plantations, was welcomed by finance and industrial capital as well as wide sections of the middle class. The nationalistic economic policies expected of the new government raised the hopes of private enterprise in Cuba that it could thereby capture a bigger slice of business.[3] Thus fragmented, the domestic opposition to the gradual nationalisation of the economy presented only a weak challenge.

By mid-February, Castro felt sufficiently confident to take over as prime minister with new, wide-ranging powers. The cabinet increasingly became a rubber stamp for policies decided by Castro and his advisers. In the summer of 1959, he moved against the moderates in the cabinet, provoked in part by Urrutia's public statements against the infiltration of Communists into the administration. Summoning the crowds once again, Castro forced Urrutia's resignation, naming a close supporter, Osvaldo Dorticós, as President in his place. The mounting tensions within the 26th July Movement over the increasing influence of the Communists reached a head with the mutiny in October of a leading rebel commander and governor of Camagüey province, Huber Matos. Once again, Castro was able to use the crisis to consolidate his power by announcing the creation of the armed militias. He also intervened in the November Congress of the Cuban Labour Federation to insist on unity between delegates of the PSP and the anti-Communist representatives of his Movement.[4] By the end of the year, the honeymoon between liberal and radical wings of the Movement was over.

Another source of tension was the growing opposition of the Church hierarchy to the radical turn of the new regime. There had been many Catholics in the anti-Batista movement and initially the Church had welcomed the Revolution. Traditionally, however, it had been a conservative force in Cuban society, having supported Spain during the Independence Wars, and later having espoused the cause of Francoism in the Spanish Civil War. When the new government began to secularise education and downgrade the institutional role of the Church in national affairs, the Catholic hierarchy joined with the anti-Castro opposition in mobilising a huge protest movement.

However, it was the increasingly virulent reaction of the US administration to Cuban reforms that accelerated the radical shift of the government. Castro had been concerned from the beginning to try to maintain relations with Washington without compromising his programme of internal reforms. In an effort to improve communications, he devoted some time during the first months of the Revolution to improving his English, which he spoke imperfectly and with a heavy Spanish accent. But there is no reason to doubt Castro's evaluation of Cuban–American relations in 1960–1 made many years later in a private conversation with an American diplomat.

I came to power with some preconceived ideas about the United States and about Cuba's relationship with her. In retrospect, I can see a number of things I wish I had done differently. We would not in any event have ended up as close friends. The US had dominated us too long. The Cuban Revolution was determined to end that domination. There was, then, an inherent conflict of interests. Still, even adversaries find it useful to maintain bridges between them. Perhaps I burned some of these bridges precipitately; there were times when I may have been more abrupt, more aggressive, than was called for by the situation. We were all younger then; we made the mistakes of youth.[5]

This unusually mild reference to the US policy towards Cuba belongs to a much later period when Castro was keen to renew relations with Washington, but it does point to two important aspects of the US–Cuban conflict. First, the revolutionary leaders knew that an accommodation with the United States was unlikely; it was therefore not the American government's over-reaction to Cuban reforms that led to the break. Second, there was an element of hot-blooded national pride in Castro's dealings with the United States that helped to precipitate the dispute. Nevertheless, for all his passion, Castro was able to exploit the conflict with the United States in order to consolidate his power and hurry the pace of the Revolution.

Castro's earliest public pronouncements on relations with the United States confirmed the economic programme of the 26th July Movement drawn up by leading moderates; Cuba, he repeatedly asserted in the first three months of the Revolution, would have a mixed economy in which American private investment and US government aid would continue to play an important role. However, it is now clear that he was already contemplating state intervention in public utilities, mining, and sugar, in all of which American interests were prominent. It is now also known that as early as March, when Urrutia's moderate government was still nominally in power, the US National Security Council was considering an option to bring down the new Cuban regime.[6] Both sides, therefore, were already preparing for a clash.

Although some form of dispute between Cuba and the United States was inevitable, it was fuelled from the beginning by mutual suspicion and misunderstanding. The initial sympathy for the Revolution among wide circles of Americans gave way to disquiet once the show trials and executions of Batista personnel involved in torture and killings began shortly after the victory. The trials, in which Castro sometimes took a leading role as prosecutor, were a more formal version of the revolutionary justice meted out to the victimisers of peasant families during the guerrilla campaign in the Sierra. American standards of justice could hardly be expected to apply to a country that had suffered years of brutal dictatorship. Similarly, when Castro announced the suspension of elections during his visit to the United States in April, few Americans could understand the extent to which parliamentary democracy in Cuba had become discredited by the corruption of the politicians of the past, with the acquiescence of the US government. The land reform law of May and the military and trade agreement signed between Cuba and the Soviet Union in February of the following year only heightened fears in the US administration that the island was turning Communist.

It should be remembered also that because of its strategic position and its historical links with the United States, Cuba had been viewed by generations of American policy-makers as a part of the defence of the southern flank of the United States, as well as a key asset in the control of the Caribbean and the shipping lanes to and from the Panama Canal. To this traditional sensitivity about security in its backyard was added the Cold War obsession with the menace of Communism which tended to obscure the essentially nationalistic roots of leftist movements in the area and indeed in other parts of the Third World.

Suspicions on the Cuban side that the United States was aiding counter-revolutionaries came to a head when a French merchant ship carrying arms blew up in Havana harbour in 4 March 1960, inflicting many casualties. In a mass rally that followed, Castro warned of the danger of an invasion by the enemies of the Cuban Revolution, issuing for the first time the famous slogan, *Patria o Muerte, Venceremos*. Indeed, less than a fortnight later, the US administration under Eisenhower secretly instructed the CIA to prepare a paramilitary force for action against the Cuban government.[7] The verbal dispute between the two countries descended into a spiral of measures and counter-measures. When the Cuban government nationalised foreign-owned petrol refineries at the end of June after they had refused to process crude oil bought from the Soviets, the US government annulled Cuba's sugar quota. The Cubans responded by seizing the larger American companies operating on the island. The United States followed with a ban on trade to Cuba. Finally, in October, Cuba nationalised not only all remaining foreign enterprises but also the larger Cuban-owned businesses.

The dynamic of the US–Cuban conflict led the revolutionary government to speed up the process of political and economic centralisation. Castro correctly judged that the looming confrontation with the United States made it possible to carry out rapidly what had been in effect a much longer-term strategy. His own assessment many years later of the events of 1960–1 is convincing:

> We were carrying out our programme little by little. All these aggressions accelerated the revolutionary process. Were they the cause? No, this would be an error. . . . In Cuba we were going to construct socialism in the most orderly possible manner, within a reasonable period of time, with the least amount of trauma and problems, but the aggressions of imperialism accelerated the revolutionary process.[8]

The crisis also polarised Cuban society. From mid-1960 the first big wave of emigrants abandoned Cuba for a life of exile in the United States. Since they were drawn largely from Cuba's business and professional elites, their departure removed a potential source of opposition to the new regime and thereby accelerated the process of political centralisation.

Finally, in April 1961, the long-expected invasion force of Cuban exiles set sail from Nicaragua under US navy escort. The new American President, John F Kennedy, had approved the invasion plan drawn up by the outgoing administration but had vetoed the use of any US forces in the combat. The landings took place on two beaches, one called Playa Girón, situated in the Bay of Pigs in the remote, swampy region of southern Matanzas; ironically, it was an area Castro had explored at length while investigating a personal project to drain the marshes. The invasion was preceded by aerial attacks on the island's air force bases by American bombers manned by exiled Cuban pilots. However, they failed to put out of action all of Cuba's tiny air force. This proved fatal to the invaders. Without authorisation to make any further air strikes and thus deprived of air support, the invading force was harassed by Cuban planes; two freighters were sunk, the CIA command ship was struck, and the rest of the fleet fled, leaving 1,300 men stranded on the two beaches. The Cuban forces moved quickly into the area under the energetic and efficient command of Castro. A photograph of the time shows him leaping off a Cuban tank in the war zone. After two days of fierce fighting, during which newly authorised air strikes inflicted heavy casualties on the Cuban militia, the invaders were overcome.

The victory at Playa Girón was celebrated amid national euphoria. It was as if the United States had finally received its due, after a century of meddling in the affairs of Cuba. Castro's prestige among the population would never be higher. Shortly before the landings, as the crisis unfolded, he had been sufficiently confident of his mass support to declare for the first time that the Revolution was a socialist revolution. Later the same year, he declared on television that he was a Marxist and that the Cuban Revolution would have a 'Marxist-Leninist' programme. The words of a popular song of the post-Playa Girón days. 'Cuba Sí, Yanquis No', suggest how collective faith in Castro seemed to override the residue of old ideologies; if Fidel was in charge, they implied, it did not matter which direction the Revolution went:

Si las cosas de Fidel
son cosas de buen marxista
que me pongan en la lista
que estoy de acuerdo con él.
(If Fidel's 'concerns' are those of a good Marxist, put
me down on the list, for I agree with him.)

The Bay of Pigs incident not only helped to define the official ideology of the Revolution but also speeded up its institutionalisation. Three months later, Castro announced the fusion of the 26th July Movement, the DR, and the Communists into the Organizaciones Integradas Revolucionarias as a first step towards the creation of a new Communist Party. It also led the Cuban leadership to seek closer ties with the Soviet Union. There was little doubt in their minds that the United States would attempt a new invasion, this time with the US marines. Castro had established a close rapport with Khrushchev in September 1960 during a United Nations General Assembly in New York; the famous embrace between the two men, the short and pudgy Soviet leader and the towering Cuban, seemed to represent a genuine mutual sympathy. Shortly afterwards a commercial and military pact had been signed between the two countries. The Soviet Union was experiencing rapid economic growth and the new sense of confidence that it gave led the Kremlin to seek to improve its position in the world balance of power by providing economic and military aid to radical Third World states. A pro-Soviet Cuba represented for Khrushchev a double opportunity: to check the growing influence of China in the Third World and above all to exert pressure on the United States. For his part, Castro was anxious to obtain substantial Soviet military aid after the Bay of Pigs to deter the United States from a second invasion attempt. Moreover, the domestic situation in 1962 was unstable; anti-government guerrillas were active in the Escambray mountains where the DR had operated during the war against Batista, the economy was floundering, and tensions had arisen in the new party between Castroists and some of the old Communists.

The idea of installing Soviet medium-range missiles on Cuban soil came, according to most accounts, from Khrushchev himself.[9] The Soviet Premier hoped thereby to strengthen his bargaining hand with Washington at a stroke. It was a move dictated by pure opportunism because the balance of nuclear deterrence at the time lay with the United States, who were hardly likely to accept the presence of nuclear warheads in their back yard. Kept in the dark about the ratio of strike power between the two superpowers, Castro evidently believed that Cuba could be drawn in under the nuclear umbrella of the Soviet Union without unleashing a world war.[10] Out of this he hoped to achieve at the least a guarantee that the United States would not invade Cuba. Furthermore, there was an important principle at stake according to Castro: Cuba's right, as a sovereign nation, to defend itself as it willed.

It is now known that by October 1962, 36 nuclear warheads had been delivered to Cuba for use with intermediate-range ballistic missiles. In addition, 9 short-range nuclear missiles with Luna launchers were ready to be used against Guantánamo in the East and Bahía Honda in the West where an amphibious invasion force was expected. These mobile 'Frog' missiles were under the command of local Soviet officers who had the discretion to launch them in the event of an invasion without consulting the supreme command in Havana or Moscow. Cuban leaders have since stressed that they fully expected an invasion and indeed, it has recently been disclosed that US troops were put on a state of high alert, while B52 bombers were prepared for an air strike and the lids of long-range missiles targeted on the Soviet Union were lifted. Moreover, some 42,000 Soviet troops were on the island, backing the 240,000 Cubans under arms.[11] Photographs taken by an American U2 spy plane revealed the presence of the intermediate-range missiles and President Kennedy demanded their withdrawal, imposing a quarantine line around the island. On 24 October, a Russian convoy including a freighter with 20 more warheads on board was steaming towards the US fleet ringing the island. The world seemed on the brink of a nuclear war. At the last moment Khrushchev pulled back. The Russian convoy turned around and headed for home. On the 27th, a US U2 plane was shot down by a Russian surface-to-air missile. But Kennedy and Khrushchev were already negotiating an end to the crisis. Without consulting Castro, the Soviet Premier agreed to remove the nuclear missiles from Cuba in exchange for the withdrawal of an ageing generation of American missiles in Turkey and a pledge that the United States would not attempt to invade Cuba.

The missile crisis of 1962 had begun as a dispute over the right of Cuba to possess offensive weapons and had ended in a superpower confrontation in which Cuba was only a pawn. By his own account, Castro was furious at being ignored in the Soviet-American negotiations. In an interview with the NBC many years later, he said this about Khrushchev's decision: 'We did not feel betrayed but we were very irritated and displeased.'[12] The resulting bad blood between Havana and Moscow was to persist throughout the sixties. Yet characteristically, Castro had gained some advantage from the whole affair. He had extracted a guarantee from the United States that, at least militarily, they would leave the Revolution in peace. At the same time he had ensured the sort of support from the Soviet Union that was indispensable if Cuba was to survive the economic siege imposed by the United States.

There can be little argument now that the actions of the US government forced Castro into a deeper military and economic reliance on the Soviet Union than he would have wished. The whole thrust of the Cuban Revolution was towards the pursuit of independence; it was above all a nationalist movement whose roots lay in a hundred-year-old anti-colonial struggle. No subsequent declarations of the friendliness of relations between the two countries have been able to disguise Cuba's dependence on its new ally. The Cuban economy began to be locked into that of the Comecon countries as effectively as it had been wedded to that of the United States, even though the form that this dependency took was very different.

✗However, it was not merely the need to survive that led Castro to side with the Soviets. In view of the bitterness of anti-US feelings among the Cuban leadership it was logical that they should feel an empathy towards the USSR as a vociferous defender of neo-colonial revolts against the United States. But there was also an ideological component in the Cuban government's turn towards Soviet-type socialism and it is this aspect that has often been misunderstood. The history of the Soviet Union offered the Cuban leaders a model of development that tied in with part of their own experience and their new position in society. After the 1917 Revolution had failed to spread to the more developed countries of Europe, the Soviet state under Stalin had abandoned the internationalist strategy of the old Bolshevik leadership and turned inwards; the theory that socialism in one country was possible became the new orthodoxy. Through a brutal process of industrialisation, the USSR had grown into a powerful, state-run economy that possessed, in its purely formal appearance, the structures of socialism though not its heart, workers' control. The transformation of a relatively underdeveloped nation into an industrial power had been carried out independently of the rest of the world under the centralised direction of the Communist Party.

Castro felt some sympathy towards Stalin, though he could hardly be described as a Stalinist himself. In an interview with an American journalist, he declared, 'Stalin had . . . great merits, extraordinary merits without a doubt, in the period of industrialization of the USSR, and at the head of the Soviet state in the difficult days of the Nazi attack.'[13] Moreover, there were other models of centralised development under a one-party system that the Cuban leaders looked to, such as North Korea and China. Castro believed that his programme of reforms required a similar centralisation of political and economic control. A return to private enterprise or even a mixed economy would mean encouraging political plurali-sation; and even if this were possible in the siege conditions imposed by the United States, it would slow down or prevent the longed-for transformation of Cuban society. But Soviet

Communism was not a model that Castro wished to implant into Cuba; he preferred rather to graft it on to the peculiar conditions of Cuban society. 'We must not ignore experience,' he said in a speech in 1966, referring to the Soviets, 'but we must also guard against a mechanical copying of formulas.'[14]

In fact, Castro was too restless and the Cuban Revolution too idiosyncratic for Soviet orthodoxy. Even after Castro's declaration of socialism on the eve of the Bay of Pigs invasion, it had taken the Kremlin leaders a year to warm to his leadership. Instead, it was a group of pre-Revolutionary Communists who seemed to have their support. Since their secret negotiations with Castro soon after the revolutionary triumph, the Communist leaders had begun to occupy prominent positions in the embryonic new state. Among them there were many who were able to adjust to the wildly unorthodox leadership of Castro and his followers; the increasing *rapprochement* with the Soviet Union no doubt smoothed the passage. But there were others who remained uneasy about Castroism and had attempted to use their position to place reliable Communists at the head of the rank-and-file organisations of the new party. In March 1962, Castro had asserted his own authority by launching into a vitriolic attack against the most prominent member of this faction, Aníbal Escalante. He accused him of packing the party with relatives and fellow members; now that Cuba was officially socialist, he was using his prestige as a Communist, according to Castro, to undermine the authority of its true leaders.[15]

In an earlier incident, during a commemoration of José Antonio Echeverría, the student leader murdered by Batista's police in 1957, the chairman had read out Echeverría's testament, omitting, under instructions from members of the faction, a passage indicating his religiosity. Castro had been following the text of the testament and leaped up to make an impassioned speech denouncing the censorship as a 'short-sighted, sectarian, stupid and defective conception, negating History'. It was, he went on, 'a miserable, cowardly, mutilated symptom or current of those who have no faith in Marxism, of those who have no faith in the Revolution, of those who have no faith in its ideas'.[16] In attacking the group of pre-Revolutionary Communists, Castro was also asserting his independence from Moscow orthodoxy. The Russian ambassador, who had been implicated in the Escalante affair, was removed on Castro's request and replaced by a man of his own choice. Henceforth, the Kremlin would have to recognise that there was only one supreme authority in Cuba.

Over the following decades, Castro's policies were to fluctuate beween orthodoxy and heterodoxy according to domestic and international circumstances. But his alignment to the USSR was not mere expedience. There were elements of Soviet orthodoxy that suited the conditions in Cuba as the Revolutionary leaders saw them: the need for state control, a disciplined workforce, the subordination of consumption to production, and a world-wide ideological church. Notions of freedom, equality, and the right of self determination that figured prominently in the official doctrine of the Soviet Union coincided with strands of the Cuban radical tradition. Indeed Castro's profession of Marxism–Leninism has been taken at face value by many commentators writing from diametrically opposed viewpoints, as if it were a stigma or a halo. Yet if the Marxist-Leninist movement was a church it was one with many heresies already. For all the attempts of Cuban historians and politicians, the Revolution cannot be squeezed into the mould of European revolutionary so- cialism. It was not directly the result of the class struggle, nor did the organised working class emerge as the new hegemonic force in Cuban society. Rather, the Revolution belongs to the movements of national liberation that swept the Third World in the post-war period. As in Cuba, they were usually led by disaffected sections of the middle class, often using the name of socialism to describe the nationalised economy and centralised state that substituted for the old regime.

However, the genesis of the Cuban Revolution was unlike that of any other Third World revolution. The most striking difference was the ease of Castro's victory. Compared to the long and bloody struggles in China, Algeria, and Vietnam, for example, the Cuban Revolution was a relatively simple business. This was due to the peculiar structural conditions of Cuban society: the political fragility of the Batista regime, the dependent status of the Cuban bourgeoisie, the small size of the island, its relatively developed urban society. It was to a great extent the facility of Castro's victory that seized the imagination of millions of people in Latin America and Europe, for whom it became a repository of hopes and fantasies. Yet far from being a universal prototype, the

Revolution was a Cuban affair that could not be duplicated elsewhere, as the revolutionary leaders were to find out to their cost. The Revolution drew its inspiration from Cuban history, and the shape that its institutions took derived from the imperatives of economic growth and social reform in the conditions of siege imposed by the United States. It was to these two fundamental issues that Castro turned in the first decade of his Revolution.

. . .

NOTES AND REFERENCES

1. Franqui C 1980 *Diary of the Cuban Revolution*. Viking Press, New York, p. 338
2. Szulc T 1987 *Fidel: a Critical Portrait*. Hutchinson, London, pp. 369–73
3. Domínguez J 1 1978 *Cuba: Order and Revolution*. Harvard University, Cambridge, MA, p. 195
4. *Bohemia*, 29 Nov. 1959; *Revolución*, 23 Nov. 1959
5. Smith W S 1987 *The Closest of Enemies*. Norton, New York, pp. 144–5
6. Szulc 1987, p. 384
7. Op. cit., p. 416
8. Op. cit., p. 384
9. Khrushchev N 1971 *Khrushchev Remembers*. Penguin, Harmondsworth, vol 1, pp. 526–7. This was confirmed by Castro in his speech to the Havana Conference on the Missile Crisis in January 1992
10. See his conversation with Szulc T 1987, pp. 470–4
11. Blight J G and Welch D A 1990 *On the Brink. Americans and Soviets Reexamine the Cuban Missile Crisis*. Noonday Press, New York; Brown University 1992 *Tripartite Conference on the October Crisis of 1962 (Havana 8–13 Jan. 1992)*; author's interview with Colonel Casteneiros, March 1992
12. Granma Weekly Review (*GWR*), 13 March 1988
13. Castro F 1977 *Fidel Castro habla con Barbara Walters*. Carlos Valencia Editores, Colombia, p. 69
14. Quoted in Dumont R 1974 *Is Cuba Socialist?* Viking Press, New York, p. 39
15. *Cuba Socialista*, May 1962
16. Op. cit., April 1962

Chapter 5

THE GRAND ILLUSION

The Cuban Revolution had all the appearance of a triumph of individual heroism. Castro's achievement in overthrowing the Batista regime and defying the United States encouraged the belief in the capacity of the will to overcome all obstacles. The relative ease of the Revolution and the immense enthusiasm of the people led Castro and his followers to believe that with the same determination and political flair the Cubans could be mobilised to triumph over the intractable problem of underdevelopment. The handicaps were immense: Cuba was a small, only partially developed island that seemed trapped by its sugar monoculture and dependent on Soviet support for its survival. Nevertheless, the battle for development and independence, fought under the banner of socialism, became Castro's central preoccupation as soon as he had won power. The swings in his policies during the first decade of his rule can only be understood in the light of this grand illusion.

At the same time, Castro's prodigious role in the Revolution led many Cubans to believe, to his dismay, that he was infallible; over the coming years, he would devote much time in his speeches to the crowds unfolding his own mistakes to public scrutiny. Even those liberals who chose to go into exile when the Revolution swung to the left could only explain events in terms of charisma, or what one of them called 'the mesmerising talents of a unique leader'.[1] Against Castro's own wishes, a cult of personality developed around his figure, but of a milder and more endearing kind than that associated with leaders of other Communist regimes. There are no icons celebrating the living heroes of the Revolution, and the congenial public image of Castro is far from the granite deification of Stalin or Kim Il Sung. Wherever he

78

goes, he is buttonholed by people. He is comrade, *caudillo*, and benefactor rolled into one.

The basis of Castro's popularity has undoubtedly been his unique relationship with the masses, whether on the television screen or in public meetings. By all accounts, he had been a good orator in his university days but his style changed radically after the Revolution. In his youth, he was prone to use the inflated rhetoric shared by politicians of the day and common to Cuban and Hispanic traditions. This grandiloquent style of oratory was filled with Biblical and literary allusions, and relied for its effect on a crescendo of antitheses and resonant epithets to rouse the crowd to action. His post-Revolutionary speeches were no less profuse and considerably longer but their purpose was generally didactic rather than agitational, reflecting Castro's new role as leader. In these speeches, Castro would strike an immediate rapport with the crowd and a kind of dialogue would ensue, in which he responded to the mood of the audience and improvised answers to comments shouted from below. Delivered at a pitch surprisingly high for such a large figure, his speeches covered a broad range of issues and he made painstaking efforts to explain his views in straightforward terms, alternating facts and lengthy statistics with jokes and everyday images close to the experience of ordinary people. In a speech to metal workers in 1967, for instance, he used the example of the famous state-produced Coppelia ice-cream to illustrate his belief in the superiority of socialist over capitalist production. Capitalism, he admitted, produces better-made goods initially but later tends to lower the quality. Socialism, on the other hand, strives constantly to improve quality. Thus, he went on, the Coppelia ice-cream factory had never ceased in its efforts to increase its range of flavours and there were now twenty.[2]

He also used the public forum as the occasion to launch campaigns against elites or individuals in the regime against whom he had turned. To the delight of the audience, he would fire off gigantic broadsides, naming his victims or pointing the finger at unnamed individuals or groups or government departments until their political reputation lay in pieces. The importance of public speech-making to Castro's exercise of power can be judged by the fact that between 1959 and 1989 he made an average of one speech every four days of a length that varied from about one hour to half a day according to the political exigencies of the time. The shortest speeches were made in the seventies when Castro consciously played a less prominent part in the government of Cuba.

Throughout the sixties, Castro devoted himself above all to the task of rousing the Cuban people for the Herculean task of development. The problems they faced, according to the Cuban leadership, were not just material but psychological. Conquering underdevelopment meant creating the New Man. In a typical Castroist reversal of Stalinist determinism, the New Man would be forged in order to raise the productive forces rather than as a consequence of their development. Indeed, this new man was supposed to be already present in the figures of the Revolutionary leaders, both men and women (though the New Woman was given considerably less prominence). The official morality of the Revolution was an extension into everyday life of that of the Sierra campaign. The new virtues that Cubans were encouraged to adopt were austerity, discipline, selflessness, and comradeship. In a speech to workers' delegates towards the end of 1959 Castro declaimed: 'In the army of the workers there must be discipline, there must be comradeship, there must be unity; you are the officers of this army, you are the leaders.'[3]

The morality of the Revolution was misunderstood by many of those on the Left abroad who saw Cuba as a model. The emphasis on austerity and discipline did not mark the birth of a new society, as they thought, but rather a return to the primitive accumulation of capital managed by the state. As Castro would reiterate for decades, the Cubans had to work doubly hard, subordinating private consumption to production in order to overcome the legacy of the past. 'We want to work hard,' said Castro in a speech much later, 'because we must work hard, because we're a Third World Country, because we lost centuries under colonialism, nearly sixty years under neocolonialism, and we've also lost a few years under the Revolution. We must make up for lost time.'[4] The regime of austerity was made all the harsher by the economic boycott of the United States and the need to divert scarce resources to national defence. The new ideology, therefore, made a virtue out of necessity.

Even more than economic reform, Castro's greatest preoccupation was to provide the human and social resources that he saw as vital to economic take-off, in particular education, health, and housing. Soon after the victory, he organised thousands of young volunteers into brigades and sent them into the countryside to teach the many illiterate people among the rural population how to read and write. This campaign became one of the Revolution's great epics because it virtually wiped out illiteracy in Cuba in a few years; it also served to socialise many Cubans in the cities and the countryside into the new values of the Revolution. State provision of a free and modern health service, an efficient educational system, and cheap new housing was seen as a political as well as an economic imperative. Providing for the basic needs of the population, so it was believed, lessened the importance of wages and reduced the demand for consumer goods.

The countryside benefited more than the cities from this state investment. The rural areas had been profoundly deprived before the Revolution. Only 15 per cent of rural inhabitants had had running water compared with 80 per cent of the urban population, and only 9 per cent of households in the countryside had had electricity. Agricultural workers had earned less than $80 a month on average (compared to the $120 that had been the average monthly industrial wage) yet they had also been chronically underemployed. State funds were now ploughed into the rural areas, providing jobs and basic facilities. Havana, on the other hand was relatively neglected, its façades fading and peeling in the damp, salty air.

Underpinning the social reforms and the moral campaign of austerity lay the belief among Castro and his closest supporters that they could force the stages of development and create in a short while the conditions for a Communist society, one in which each person received according to his or her needs and gave according to his or her capacity. Orthodox Marxism insisted that without the development of productive forces on a massive scale not even socialism was possible; underdevelopment or semi-development meant the persistence of capitalist relations of production in one guise or another whatever the degree of nationalisation of the economy. Che Guevara, the most articulate exponent among the Castroists of the belief in socialism here and now, argued on the contrary that Cuba's alignment with the developed Soviet bloc made it possible to jump stages in the transition towards socialism.[5]

The Bolshevik leaders had faced a similar dilemma in 1924. Surrounded on all sides by hostile states and confronted with the resistance of the mass of peasants to any socialist measures, they had engaged in a bitter polemic about how to save the Revolution. One wing had argued for a policy of rapid industrialisation, accumulating the capital to carry this out by subordinating consumption to production and eroding private rural capital. Fearing the collapse of agriculture and a counter-revolution led by the richer peasantry, another wing of the Bolsheviks favoured a policy of allowing the peasants to grow wealthy and thus of using private enterprise to reconstruct Russia. Stalin had supported the second option at first, and once he had seized power put the first into operation by destroying the peasantry.

The Cuban leaders believed they faced none of these problems; economic alliance with the Soviet bloc allowed industrialisation to take place without trauma, they felt, while the Cuban peasantry actually supported socialist land reform. Under the direction of Che Guevara as Minister for Industry, ambitious plans were drawn up to industrialise Cuba without sacrificing the living standards of the Cubans. Indeed, the first two years saw a rise in consumption as the poorer sections of the population gained access to better food and housing. This redistribution was possible in part because of the smooth passage of the Revolution; the economy had not been damaged by civil war, the factories were well-stocked and equipped, foreign reserves from previous exports were still available. But it soon became clear that the economy could not sustain such relatively high levels of consumption; stocks were running out, cattle were being destroyed to be eaten, and the economic blockade by the United States could not be circumvented by trade with the Soviet bloc. In March 1962, rationing was introduced for the first time; Cubans would have to live with it from then on.

At the same time, the hope that the Cuban economy could somehow be plugged into that of the Comecon countries was eroded by two major problems: the sheer physical distance involved; and the incompatibility of Cuba's industry and infrastructure, until then geared to the US economy, with those of the Soviet bloc. Moreover, neither Comecon technology nor its technicians were up to the same standard as those of the United States. A combination of inexperience and poor quality of ráw materials and machines led to many failures in the programme of industrialisation. Despite the wildly optimistic forecasts of Castro and others, industry grew by only 0.4 per cent in 1962 and actually declined by 1.5 per cent in the following year. Agriculture suffered even more, not only as a result of the emphasis on industrialisation but also because of massive and not always successful attempts to diversify produce. The sugar industry, already in a parlous state under Batista, had been hit by the loss of many of its managers and technicians who had begun to emigrate to the United States a year or so after the Revolutionary triumph. Moreover, in the rush to diversify agriculture, many canefields had been burnt down; the 1963 harvest turned out to be the worst since the Second World War. According to government statistics, sugar production dropped from a post-Revolutionary peak of 6,876,000 metric tons in 1961 to 3,883,000 in 1963, while the index of total agricultural production fell to its lowest level since the forties and industrial production suffered a steep decline.[6] These problems were compounded by the economic disruption caused by structural change as well as the diversion of resources towards defence. By the middle of 1963, the Cuban economy was heading for a slump.

The crisis brought out latent divisions within the Cuban leadership. Both Castro and Guevara had been the exponents of the Stalinist model of industrialisation and agricultural diversification. This process of modernisation was to be managed entirely by a centralised leadership allocating targets and controlling budgets. At the head of this vast operation as Minister of Industry, Guevara spent most of the day and night receiving reports, launching schemes, handling accounts, poring over technical books, acting in his new role much as he had done as a guerrilla in the Sierra. Similarly, Castro tirelessly roamed the Cuban countryside, setting up ambitious agricultural projects, getting labour and machinery moved around, animating and lecturing his people wherever he went. The French agronomist René Dumont, who spent a short time with Castro as an adviser, wrote about his experience: 'Travelling with Castro I sometimes had the impression that I was visiting Cuba with its owner, who was showing off its fields and pastures, its cows if not its men.'[7] For the old Communists, the whole style of the Revolutionary leadership must have seemed chaotic. Moreover, reformist breezes were beginning to blow from Eastern Europe counselling a very different economic management to the one practised by the Castroists.

The internal debate that ensued in Cuba was similar to that among Bolshevik leaders in 1925 and the Chinese Communists in 1958–9 after the débâcle of the Great Leap Forward. The pre-Revolutionary Communists and their allies in economic policy argued that a primitive accumulation of capital was only possible on the basis of a large increase in sugar production. Only the mass export of sugar and a better use of its derivatives, in their opinion, could create the platform for economic take-off. At the same time, they favoured the new reforms sweeping Eastern Europe, providing for internal economic autonomy and a greater stress on profitability and material incentives. Their polemical interventions were tacitly directed against Guevara as the most conspicuous backer of existing economic policy, but Castro's support for Guevara's ideas was well known.[8] Always a pragmatist, however, Castro gave way in the face of the economic setbacks of 1963–4. The shift in policy, moreover, was urged by the Soviet leaders who offered to coat the bitter pill by guaranteeing a market for Cuban sugar at a high fixed price that allowed for long-term planning. Guevara's ministry was split up, resources were diverted from industry to agriculture, and a bloodletting began of officials in the bureaucracy.

As they would continue to do in the coming decades, the Cuban leaders sought to blame individuals rather than policies or the policy-making mechanisms for the collapse of the industrialisation venture. It was clear that the plans of Castro, Guevara, and their closest followers had been over-ambitious. Reflecting on this period many years later, Castro confessed, 'At that time we had many ideas that were well-intentioned, but they were not very realistic; we wanted to jump stages.'[9] One problem was that the success of the Revolution created a faith that revolutionary consciousness or *conciencia* could move mountains. In a characteristically honest vein, Guevara concluded, 'We did not base our arguments on statistical facts, nor on historical experience. We dealt with nature in a subjective manner, as if by talking to it we could persuade it.'[10] Cuban workers and technicians were willing, indeed almost too willing, but on the whole they lacked the necessary experience and technical knowledge. Another problem was the extreme centralisation of decision-making, as a result of which the Cuban economy suffered severe dislocations. In this Castro was as much to blame as Guevara, since he was responsible for launching numerous agricultural initiatives like military offensives which, by his own later admission, failed to take into account cost effectiveness or appropriate technology.[11]

Nevertheless, it was Guevara who bore the consequences of the débâcle, though he remained for a short while as close as ever to Castro. Eighteen months after the decision to overhaul economic policy was announced, Guevara left for a tour of African and Asian countries and on his return resigned his government positions and gave up his Cuban citizenship. In June 1965, he left for Africa with a small force of veterans of the Sierra campaign to assist the Katangese rebels against the Congolese government, and in the following year, he set up a guerrilla nucleus in Bolivia in an attempt to repeat the Cuban success.

Guevara's departure from Cuba has been the subject of much discussion. It seems probable that he left simply because there was no obvious role for him once his policy of industrialisation had failed. He was not sacked, nor is it likely that he quarrelled with Castro since the latter was shortly to revive many of Guevara's most cherished policies. Besides, it was typical of Castro's leadership to move aside rather than to move out any leading exponent of a policy that had officially been declared a failure. However, Guevara's unorthodox methods and his growing criticism of the Soviet Union's policies in the Third World ill suited the delicate process of *rapprochement* with Moscow made necessary by the economic crisis. At the same time, Guevara had always made clear that his overriding commitment was to revolution in the South American continent. The example of the Cuban Revolution offered the hope that similar guerrilla actions could succeed elsewhere; the new mood of rebellion stirring in the Third World in the mid-sixties, stimulated by the resistance of the Vietnamese against the United States, further encouraged his grand vision.

Guevara's disappearance and the collapse of the industrialisation campaign strengthened the hand of the orthodox, pro-Soviet elements in the middle stratum of the Cuban leadership. Indeed, it seemed for a while as if Castro was bowing to greater pressure. The price of renewed Soviet support was a certain decentralisation of economic decision-making and the introduction of a limited range of market mechanisms. At the same time, the Cuban leaders hastened the process of creating an orthodox institutional framework urged by the Kremlin, and in October 1965, the single party of the Revolution, the Cuban Communist Party (PCC), was formed out of the organisations that had emerged from the victory.

Yet Castro had not abandoned the twin objectives of the Revolution: to create a Communist society on the basis of a developed economy, and to secure a lasting independence for Cuba. Soviet policies since the missile crisis increasingly seemed to threaten the achievement of these objectives. On a domestic plane, the new economic reforms in the Soviet Union were incompatible with the model propounded by Castro of a society struggling to survive and develop. In his eyes, the central task of the Cubans was to accumulate resources under the direction of the Revolutionary elite, who would cream off the surplus to pay for defence and industrial investment while maintaining egalitarian distribution and essential social services such as health and education. Through the introduction of material incentives, the reforms threatened to divert the efforts of Cubans towards personal material goals rather than national accumulation. In any case, monetary rewards made little sense in a domestic economy offering few consumer goods and a relatively high social wage. The Soviet reforms also threatened to confine the Cuban economy to a specialised niche within the Comecon system, producing sugar and tropical products in exchange for industrial goods; this would merely renew a neo-colonial relationship long familiar to Cuba, though in a different guise. The new economic model recently adopted by the Soviet Union also laid open the Cuban political system to emerging elites in the bureaucracy and among workers who would not only create inequalities but stand between the leadership and the masses.

On an international plane, the Soviet Union's policies also seemed to pose serious difficulties for the Cuban Revolution. The twentieth Congress of the Soviet Communist Party in 1956 had declared that the new balance of power between East and West created the conditions for a peaceful emergence of socialism in the West in ways determined by the local characteristics of each country; Communist Parties had thus been given the green light to take the parliamentary road to socialism. This meant the adoption of a new form of Popular Frontism; that is, an alliance with forces ranged against local oligarchies stretching from social democrats to reformist generals. It also entailed the development of a new relationship with Third World countries characterised by a greater concern for commercial viability and less for the political colour of governments. The decision had marked the beginning of a new era of peaceful coexistence with the West, disrupted briefly by the missile crisis of 1962.

Both the Chinese and the Cuban leadership disliked the policy of peaceful coexistence and the parliamentary road to socialism. For over half a century constitutional methods had failed to bring about reform in Cuba. In Latin America, when elected governments had attempted to introduce social and economic changes, they had been threatened and, in Guatemala's case, destroyed by US-sponsored counter-revolution. Both the Chinese and the Cuban Revolutions had been the result of guerrilla campaigns starting in the countryside and spreading to the cities. For the Castroists conditions were ripe in Latin America for such actions, which would culminate in a continent-wide revolution. In a barely disguised attack on the Latin American Communist Parties, Castro declared in 1966 that guerrilla struggle was the only revolutionary road that most countries in that continent could take.

> What we are convinced about is that in the immense majority of Latin American nations conditions exist for making the Revolution that are far superior to those that existed in Cuba, and that if those revolutions are not being made in those countries it is because many who call themselves revolutionaries lack conviction.[12]

Indeed, in the mid-sixties, the international situation suggested to the Cuban leaders that this course was essential for the survival of the Revolution. Castro was dismayed by the Sino-Soviet dispute which served only to weaken the socialist bloc. 'Not even the attacks on North Vietnam [by the United States],' he said in a speech in March 1965, 'have helped to overcome the divisions within the socialist family. . . . Who benefits from these disputes other than our enemies?'[13] Cuba's close proximity to the United States made it extremely vulnerable, and the Cubans were not confident about the assurances given to Moscow at the end of the missile crisis that the United States would not try to invade the island. The Sino–Soviet split, added to the new moderation of the Soviet Union especially after the fall of Khrushchev in 1965, appeared only to encourage the United States to greater aggression, of which their growing intervention in Vietnam was the clearest sign. Moscow could not be relied on to defend the Cuban Revolution; this had been the traumatic lesson of 1962. Besides, the Soviet Union seemed increasingly conciliatory towards the United States. The Cuban Revolution needed Soviet aid but it could only survive in the long run through the massive efforts of its people to create the material basis for development and through the export of its model to Latin America where, it was hoped, new revolutions would come to the aid of the beleaguered island.

For Castro, therefore, the Soviet Union's policies in the mid-sixties represented neither a guarantee of defence against the United States nor a model of economic development. At the same time he could not afford to lose the support of Moscow. This dilemma lay behind the swings in his policy in the second half of the sixties. From 1965, Castro began to distance himself from the Soviet Union and openly to criticise its foreign policy in terms even harsher than those used by Guevara. While in the early years of the Revolution he had defied the Eagle, he could be said now to be baiting the Bear. At home, he launched a new offensive to tackle the problem of underdevelopment once and for all, sweeping aside the faint-hearted, the non-conformists, and above all the residual pro-Soviet opposition within the PCC. The two campaigns were part of the same overall objective: to defend the Revolution, to assert Cuban independence, and to mobilise the people for the task of development. The failure of the industrialisation programme made the whole project all the more urgent.

Castro's assertiveness towards Moscow derived from a new sense of confidence. While the Sino–Soviet dispute had weakened the socialist bloc it also gave Cuba a certain leverage over the Soviet Union, which was anxious to keep

Cuba on its side of the divide. Castro was careful, however, to keep his distance from the Chinese, who were trying to exploit the differences between Havana and Moscow.[14] The lukewarm support given to North Vietnam by both the Chinese and the Soviet Union raised the possibility of a third alignment of socialist forces embracing Hanoi, the Vietcong, the Cubans, and North Korea. The resistance of the North Vietnamese under the onslaught of American bombs must have been a source of immense encouragement to the Cuban leaders. Moreover, Cuba enjoyed the sort of prestige among Third World nations and in many sections of public opinion in the West that Moscow could hardly ignore.

But Castro's confidence rested above all on his faith in the strategy of guerrilla warfare in Latin America. In the early sixties it seemed as if the Cuban example could be exported. There was widespread agitation among peasants in Central America and in the Andean region. Guerrilla groups had sprung up in Colombia, Venezuela, Peru, and Guatemala. And in Bolivia, the poorest, roughest, and most central nation in South America, Guevara was preparing to launch a guerrilla war calculated to spread to neighbouring Argentina, Brazil, Peru, and beyond. His presence in the Bolivian jungle with a select group of veterans of the Sierra campaign led to exaggerated hopes of a revolutionary wave in the sub-continent that would end Cuba's isolation and lessen its dependence on the Soviet Union. Even Castro seemed to have succumbed to the myth to which the Cuban Revolution had given birth that heroism or conviction could triumph over all odds. The Cuban Revolution would not have taken place, he said in a speech in 1966, if account had been taken of objective conditions. 'As for subjective conditions,' he went on, 'there were possibly no more than twenty, at first no more than ten, people who believed that a revolution was possible . . . what was important was not the individuals involved but conviction; merit lies not in the individuals but in conviction.'[15]

Castro's barely disguised attacks on the Soviet Union between 1965 and 1968 can only be understood in the light of this confidence that a new revolutionary axis was taking shape, led by Cuba, Vietnam, and North Korea, and soon embracing newly liberated Latin American countries and several Third World nations; it was to be a new Communist front that would turn the tide of American imperialism to which the Soviets and their orthodox followers seemed to have capitulated. This was the hidden agenda of the Tricontinental Conference of revolutionary organisations from Africa, Asia, and Latin America held in Havana in January 1966, during which a message from Guevara was read out calling on Latin American revolutionaries to set up 'two, three, many Vietnams'. Some eighteen months later, this was followed by a Cuban-sponsored meeting of Latin American revolutionary organisations in which a new front was set up, the Latin American Solidarity Organisation (the acronym in Spanish, OLAS, means 'waves'). Against the votes of the few orthodox Communist Parties that attended the meeting, OLAS approved the strategy of guerrilla warfare and elected the absent Guevara, at the time deep in the Bolivian highlands, as honorary president. During the conference, Castro launched into an attack on the Venezuelan Party for sabotaging the guerrilla movement in that country and for intriguing against Cuba. He also criticised the Soviet Union for delivering petrol and granting credit to countries that had imposed a trade boycott on Cuba.

Moscow reacted to its increasingly wayward and captious protégé by delaying the signing of trade agreements, and eventually cutting back on urgent supplies of oil to Cuba. Soviet–Cuban relations reached a low point when Castro refused to attend the celebration of the fiftieth anniversary of the Russian Revolution in autumn 1967. A few weeks later, he delivered his most stinging attack on Communist orthodoxy. At an international conference of intellectuals in Havana, he proclaimed,

> there can be nothing so anti-Marxist as dogma, there can be nothing so anti-Marxist as the petrification of ideas. And there are ideas that are even put forward in the name of Marxism that seem real fossils . . . Marxism needs to develop, overcome a certain sclerosis, interpret the realities of the present in an objective and scientific way, behave like a revolutionary force and not like a pseudo-revolutionary church.[16]

This audacious message, however, was directed mainly at those in the ranks of the Party in Cuba who had misgivings about the radical direction which the Revolution was taking. In February 1968, barely a month after Castro's speech, the leading exponents of Soviet orthodoxy were put on trial accused of factionalism. The report of the Central Committee outlining the charges was introduced by Raúl Castro and lasted twelve hours. It unfolded a lurid tableau of secret gatherings among pro-Soviet Communists and clandestine rendezvous with Soviet and Eastern European officials.[17] That the so-called 'microfaction' affair amounted to a serious conspiracy is doubtful but it exposed the continuing tensions between the two wings of the Cuban Revolution, the pre-Revolutionary Communists and the 26th July Movement. The trial also served to warn the Soviets that they would not be allowed to indulge in internal lobbying.

The crackdown against the pro-Soviet Communists was part of a broader offensive launched in 1968 by Castro to bend the will of the Cubans to the task of accumulation. Since the reorganisation of the economic ministries in 1965, he had taken over the reins of the economy as President of INRA, personally approving and directing scores of ambitious projects. The East European model of five-year central planning was abandoned in favour of regional or sectoral plans orchestrated by individual leaders such as Castro himself. By the beginning of 1968, however, there were ominous signs that the economy was heading for a crisis once again. The Soviet Union was tightening the screw by drastically reducing its supply of fuel and gas oil to Cuba. Many of the economic plans had failed to live up to expectations owing to inadequate planning or lack of technical expertise.[18] Castro was particularly irked by the operations of small farmers and traders who were taking advantage of rationing and commodity shortages to run a black market. Their presence was not politically expedient at a time when he was calling for universal sacrifice nor did it correspond to the society that he was attempting to build. 'We did not make a revolution,' he exclaimed, 'in order to establish the right to trade.' Seizing with vivid detail on the example of street stall-holders who sold fried egg sandwiches, he warned of the danger of allowing small-scale private capitalism to expand.[19] In March, he launched a Revolutionary Offensive to mop up the last vestiges of the private sector, nationalising over 55,000 small businesses accounting for around a third of Cuba's retail sales.[20]

The harsher political climate was reflected in the growing

campaign against Cubans who did not conform to the spirit of discipline urged by Castro. As early as 1965 the army had begun forcibly to recruit gays into separate work battalions. Privately, Castro was known for sharing the typically Cuban male prejudice against homosexuals. An ex-Castroist recounts hearing the two Castro brothers laughing at a joke about a Czech homosexual-detection machine.[21] But after a plea by the Writers' and Artists' Union, several of whose members had been press-ganged into the battalions, he had ordered them to be disbanded in 1967.[22] Increasingly, intellectuals and creative artists were also coming under fire, in particular from the military, for failing to produce exemplary works rather in the style laid down by Stalin's Minister of Culture Zhdanov.[23] Castro had originally defined the role of the intellectual in the Cuban Revolution at a meeting with artists and writers in 1961 in which he had established the principle that everything was permissible within the Revolution but nothing against it. However, this was interpreted by a growing band of neo-Stalinists in the bureaucracy and military as ruling out anything but socialist realism. Artists and writers who appeared to express doubts about the Revolution or whose creative activity ignored political correctness began to find it progressively harder to have their work approved. *Lunes*, the iconoclastic cultural supplement of the official newspaper, *Revolución* was closed down in 1961. By the late sixties, a number of intellectuals had been forced into exile while others had been jailed or compelled publicly to confess their 'counter-revolutionary views'.

It is difficult to establish Castro's precise attitude towards the persecution of wayward intellectuals. He may not have approved of the over-zealous application of socialist realism, and many years later he joined in the retrospective criticism of the cultural line of the sixties and early seventies.[24] But there could be little doubt concerning his general position in the debate about cultural and educational policies. In the early days of the new regime, there had been differences among teachers, intellectuals and cultural officials about the nature of Revolutionary art and education. For some, the Revolution represented the liberation of the creative and critical spirit; for others, art and education had to serve political priorities. For Castro, the intellectual had to be at the service of the 'people', subordinating his or her own individuality to the needs of the Revolution. Castro may have shared this neo-Zhdanovism with the old Cuban Stalinists who had now gained influence in the regime but in his case it sprang perhaps from different sources. The years of conspiratorial activity and guerrilla struggle had imbued him with a militaristic distrust of ideological or cultural pluralism. Because of his own social background, he had never identified with the cosmopolitan culture of many of his fellow students in Havana. Moreover in his own personal relations, Castro had shown a strong vein of prudishness. During his stay in Mexico, according to a close friend and supporter, he had got engaged briefly to a beautiful Cuban girl and, infuriated by the fact that she wore a bikini when going swimming, he insisted that she wore a bathing suit that he bought especially for her.[25] This underlying puritanism extended to political and cultural matters as well, taking the guise of an unavoidable austerity. Castro's speeches in the late sixties argued that the very survival of the Revolution depended on the total commitment of every Cuban to its immediate objectives; any other attitude, he implied, was a dangerous diversion. This message was spelt out in September 1968 in a speech to the local Committees for the Defence of the Revolution. Reviewing the difficult economic situation he exhorted:

> And we repeat: no liberalism! No softening! A revolutionary nation, an organised nation, a combative nation, a strong nation, because these are the virtues that are required these days. And everything else is pure illusion, it would be to underestimate the task, underestimate the enemy, underestimate the historic importance of this period, underestimate the struggle that lies ahead of us.[26]

The urgent tone of his speech reflected the fact that by 1968 Castro's options were narrowing. On one hand, the guerrilla movements in Latin America were collapsing. In October 1967, after a harrowing time in the Bolivian mountains, Guevara and his group had been captured and murdered by American-trained Bolivian Rangers. His death was a double blow to Castro. Aside from his personal grief at the loss of a close friend and comrade, the failure of the Bolivian venture cast doubt on the possibility of exporting the Cuban model of guerrilla warfare to the South American continent. Despite Castro's words that it was ideas not individuals that counted, the death of Guevara was all the more a defeat for the guerrilla strategy because of the mystique of invulnerability that surrounded the living heroes of the Cuban Revolution.

Castro laid much of the blame for Guevara's death on the shoulders of the Bolivian Communist Party, whose leaders he accused of sabotaging the guerrilla operation.[27] Yet this only underlined the difficulty of working independently of the orthodox Parties which in several countries controlled resources vital to the success of the guerrillas. Moreover, at the end of the sixties the policies of the popular front advocated by the Communist Parties seemed about to be vindicated. In Peru, a reformist, anti-oligarchic, military junta took control in 1968 and began to nationalise US multinational companies. A year later, the new democratic government of Bolivia expropriated the Gulf Oil corporation, while in Chile a broad front of parties of the left and centre-left, Popular Unity, was formed to contest the 1970 Presidential elections. In short, events in Latin America at the end of the decade seemed in themselves to counsel a return to Soviet orthodoxy on the part of the Cuban regime.

However, it was above all economic pressures that drove Castro to seek a *rapprochement* with the Soviet Union. Apart from Moscow's increasing restriction of oil supplies, the Cuban economy was in massive debt to the Soviet bloc. In the trade agreements between the two countries, the Soviet Union bought Cuban sugar at a price usually higher than that of the world market while Cuba used the non-convertible currency with which the sugar was paid for to buy Comecon oil and industrial goods. Any surplus of sugar could then be sold on the world market to raise the foreign currency vital for the purchase of technology and goods unavailable in the socialist bloc. Throughout the sixties, however, Cuban exports of sugar to the Soviet Union had been well below its imports of Comecon goods and Moscow had so far been willing to finance these trade deficits. By 1969, Cuba was about 7.5 million tons in arrears and Castro declared it to be the Year of Decisive Endeavour during which the efforts of all Cubans would be devoted to producing a harvest of 10 million tons of sugar. Whether such a record harvest could be achieved or not, Castro could no longer afford to antagonise the Soviet Union. The Warsaw Pact intervention in Czechoslovakia on 21 August 1968 gave him an unusual opportunity to begin rebuilding bridges with Moscow.

Castro's address to the Cuban nation forty-eight hours after the invasion was awaited with great expectation. A group of top Cuban officials on a visit to Europe promised the French journalist K S Karol that it 'would open a new page in the history of the international labour movement'.[28] Quite apart from Castro's growing quarrel with the Soviet Union since 1965, the Warsaw Pact invasion cannot fail to have evoked parallels with the United States' continual intervention in Cuban affairs since the island won its independence in 1902. A similar doctrine of collective security and 'spheres of influence' was being used to justify the violation of Czechoslovakia's sovereignty. And indeed, Castro began his address by dismissing the Soviet Union's claims that the intervention was legally justified. 'What cannot be denied here,' he said, 'is that the sovereignty of the Czechoslovak State was violated. . . . And the violation was, in fact, of a flagrant nature.' Nevertheless, he insisted, the intervention was a necessary evil: 'we had no doubt that the political situation in Czechoslovakia was deteriorating and going downhill on its way back to capitalism and that it was inexorably going to fall into the arms of imperialism'. In the name of the law he described as even more sacred to Communists than international law – that is, the 'people's struggle against imperialism' – the socialist bloc had been obliged to step in.

Yet Castro also used the occasion to make two tacit demands of the Soviet Union: an end to the market economy reforms in the socialist bloc, and a commitment that it would come to the defence of other socialist countries such as Cuba should they be threatened by imperialism. These demands took the form of questions:

> Does this [the intervention] by chance mean that the Soviet Union is also going to curb certain currents in the field of economy that are in favour of putting increasingly greater emphasis on mercantile relations. . .? . . . We ask ourselves . . . will they send the divisions of the Warsaw Pact to Cuba if the Yankee imperialists attack our country, or even in the case of the threat of a Yankee imperialist attack on our country, if our country requests it?[29]

Castro's qualified approval of the Czechoslovak invasion confused or disappointed many on the Left abroad who had welcomed first the Cuban Revolution and then the Prague Spring as the same break with post-Stalinist orthodoxy. It was seen then and is still seen by many commentators as a piece of *realpolitik* dictated by Soviet pressure.[30] But if it is viewed in the light of the Cuban regime's domestic problems, Castro's support for the invasion takes on a new dimension. The Czech leaders' reforms, as Castro himself argued, were an intensification of the decentralising measures and market mechanisms introduced by the Soviet Union during the mid-sixties. The 'microfaction' trial had been directed precisely against the local proponents of such measures while the Revolutionary Offensive of March had set out to eliminate the residual private sector and the budding black market that threatened to reintroduce market values into Cuba by the back door.

In Castro's eyes, no relaxation of central control and social discipline was possible in the midst of economic crisis and imperialist encirclement, as his speech at the time had made clear. The Prague Spring, luxuriating in alternative cultures, was the antithesis of his model for a besieged Cuba. The reformist measures of Dubcek and his allies had raised too many expectations and had been followed by a wave of strikes. Castro's inclination, as he was to show repeatedly over the coming years, was not to ignore social discontent but to appropriate it, to channel it in the direction he chose, to use it to undermine or displace those he believed stood in the way of the changing priorities of the Revolution. His distrust of the Prague Spring was all the deeper because its leading lights – students, artists, and intellectuals – were from the same social elite that in Cuba during the late sixties was being criticised for harbouring bourgeois liberal tendencies. Castro's lack of sympathy or understanding for the aims of the reform movement in Czechoslovakia was summed up in his dismissive remark, 'And for the thousands of millions of human beings who . . . are still living without hope under conditions of starvation and extreme want there are questions in which they are more interested than the problem of whether or not to let their hair grow.'[31]

Castro had his own reasons, therefore, for supporting the Warsaw Pact invasion. Much as he had criticised the Soviets' foreign policy, he clearly felt encouraged by their new deter-mination to prevent any further divisions within the socialist bloc that would leave Cuba dangerously exposed. At the same time, he welcomed the intervention in so far as it restored political cohesion in Eastern Europe and brought to an end a disruptive experiment in economic reform originating in the Soviet Union. In any case, Castro had little option other than to support the Soviet action. Increasingly isolated abroad, its guerrilla strategy in tatters, and saddled with a massive trade deficit, the Cuban regime could not afford to lose Soviet support.

In these circumstances, the 1969–70 campaign to produce a sugar harvest of 10 million tons became for Castro and the Revolutionary leadership a last, almost desperate attempt to accumulate the resources to develop the island and to retain a measure of independence in the formulation of their policies. In the words of the leading pre-Revolutionary Communist and head of foreign relations, Carlos Rafael Rodríguez, 'The ten million ton harvest will guarantee our country's second liberation.'[32] The campaign was also to be the apotheosis of Castro's model of mobilisation, proof that moral determination could move mountains. On its success, he staked his own reputation and that of the regime. The whole nation was roused for the task, and all other economic activity was subordinated to its achievement. Indeed, the 10 million ton harvest became a political rather than an economic goal. In a speech on 18 October 1969, Castro declared,

> The ten million ton harvest represents far more than tons of sugar, far more than an economic victory; it is a test, a moral commitment for this country. And precisely because it is a test and a moral commitment we cannot fall short by even a single gram of these ten million tons. . . . Ten million tons less a single pound – we declare it before all the world – will be a defeat, not a victory.[33]

The campaign was also designed to raise the morale of the Cubans at a time when the strains of work and rationing were beginning to surface. Workers increasingly had had to forgo the wage benefits they had won at the beginning of the Revolution in exchange for a limited range of free state services. Unpaid overtime, or 'voluntary labour' had become compulsory, while material incentives were being replaced by moral incentives such as the privileges extended to exemplary workers who formed part of the Advanced Workers' Movement. Productivity was not rising but absenteeism was. It seemed as though Castro was hoping that the great sugar campaign would reawaken the Playa Girón spirit and make hardship bearable.

In his customary style, Castro set an example to the nation by spending four hours a day during harvest time cutting cane. The planting and harvesting season was extended to increase the yield, and the celebration of Christmas was postponed.

But as the months advanced it became clear that the target would not be reached. In May 1970, Castro conceded that the harvest would fall short of the 10 million tons. In the event, the sugar yield reached a record level of around 8.5 million tons. This was indeed a remarkable achievement, almost double the amount harvested in the previous year. The failure to reach the target had been due not to a lack of willingness on the part of Cubans but to insufficient planning and inadequate technical resources. But because Castro had made the campaign a test of the credibility of the regime, the shortfall was a terrible defeat for his leadership. To make matters worse, the concentration on the harvest had resulted in severe dislocations of an economy already in crisis. Over 21 per cent of industrial and agricultural goods and more than 41 per cent of forestry products registered their worst year since the Revolution.[34]

On 26 July 1970, the anniversary of the Moncada action, Castro rose before an immense crowd to deliver one of the most important speeches of his career. Without preamble, he launched into an astonishing criticism of the management of Cuban society over the previous decade. Referring to the regime's attempt simultaneously to raise living standards and accumulate capital, he said,

> we proved incapable of waging what we called the simultaneous battle. And in effect, the heroic effort to raise production, to raise our purchasing power resulted in dislocations in the economy, in a fall in production in other sectors, and in general in an increase in our difficulties.

After running through a long list of economic indices, Castro continued, 'We are going to begin by pointing out the responsibility of all of us [leaders] and mine in particular for all these problems.' He then made a rather rhetorical proposal that the Cuban people should look for a new leadership, to which the crowd predictably shouted their dissent, and as if ashamed by this demagogic lapse, Castro admitted that it would be hypocritical on his part to pretend he wished to resign.

Nevertheless, he went on,

> I believe that we, the leaders of this Revolution, have cost too much in our apprenticeship. And unfortunately, our problem is . . . the result of our own ignorance. . . Most of the time we fell into the error of minimising the

complexity of the problems facing us. We must renew [the leadership] because it's only logical that there are comrades who are worn out, burnt out; they have lost their energy, they can no longer carry the burden on their shoulders.

Having criticised the leadership, Castro then went on to outline the changes he wanted to see. He called for more democratic consultation at a rank-and-file level. He also argued for a greater delegation of powers among the Party leadership and a profound re-examination of the whole direction of the Revolution. Recalling the assault on Moncada, the guerrilla war, and the Playa Girón invasion, he remarked,

> It is easier to win twenty wars than win the battle of development. The fight today is not against people – unless they are ourselves – we are fighting against objective factors; we are fighting against the past, we are fighting with the continued presence of this past in the present, we are fighting against limitations of all kinds. But sincerely this is the greatest challenge that we have had in our lives and the greatest challenge the Revolution has ever faced.[35]

Castro's speech was a *tour de force*, at once highly personal, didactic, and normative. There can have been few other examples of a head of state who has so explicitly revealed his own shortcomings and failures. By doing so, Castro was able to turn a defeat almost into a virtue. But his speech also marked the end of an era. It was significant that he had to return to the rostrum just after he had finished speaking because he had forgotten that part of his speech dealing with the memory of Che Guevara. Indeed, the whole Guevarist model of "burning" the stages of growth through moral mobilisation to which Castro had returned in the mid-sixties was now being quietly buried. Its failure was not so much the consequence of the abortive sugar campaign or of Soviet pressure but of a growing crisis within Cuban society. Despite the crowd's adulation of Castro, there were signs of discontent about the direction the Revolution was taking.

The clearest indication that something was wrong was the epidemic of absenteeism throughout the country; Castro himself noted that in August and September 1970, some 20 per cent of the workforce were absent on any given day, while in Oriente in August 1970 52 per cent of agricultural workers failed to show up for work.[36] It was clear that Castro's oratorical relationship with the masses and his almost daily contact with ordinary people were no substitute for an organised system of consultation. The low levels of productivity indicated also that moral incentives were not working and that many workers no longer responded to constant appeals to patriotism. There was an evident disjuncture between the great campaigns such as the 10 million ton harvest to which the Cubans had responded wholeheartedly and the daily effort of productivity. Moreover, it appeared that the free services which the regime now provided in health care, education, transport, social security, and even local telephone calls, were not enough to compensate for the lack of goods in the shops and the discomforts of everyday life.

The failure of the sugar campaign also eroded the widespread myth of Castro's infallibility. For the first time, he was seen to be vulnerable to error. Characteristically, he was able to turn this to good account by encouraging the Cubans to look for collective solutions rather than heroes and scapegoats. 'It would be an unforgivable deception of the people,' he said in his July 1970 speech, 'if we tried to pretend that the problems we have are problems here of individuals. . . . We believe that this is a problem involving the whole people!'[37] But Castro himself was to a great extent to blame for the personalism that so dominated the Cuban political system. In his frequent criticisms of bureaucracy and production problems, as well as his attacks on refractory elements in the regime, he had fostered the idea that it was individuals who were at fault and not systems or decision-making processes.

More importantly, he had encouraged the notion of emulation, highlighting the exemplary role of the heroes of the Revolution. He himself had chosen to play a pre-eminent role in Cuban affairs, not out of thirst for power, as most detractors of the Revolution would have us believe, but out of impatience. Implicit in many of his speeches was the idea that to carry out the great task of development the Cubans could not be left to their own devices because they had been conditioned by decades of neo-colonialism, not to say centuries of underdevelopment and dependency. This mentality of underdevelopment was what Castro meant when he referred in his July speech to the 'continued presence of the past in the present'. The need for exemplary leadership rather than delegation of power had been all the more acute in his eyes because the Revolution was under siege. It was rather more unusual, however, for Castro to admit that he was himself part of that tradition. In his speech to the First Congress of the Cuban Communist Party in 1975, he would admit, 'The embryo of chauvinism and of the petty-bourgeois spirit affecting those of us who reached the road of revolution by a merely intellectual way develops, sometimes unconsciously, certain attitudes that may be regarded as self-sufficiency and excessive self-esteem.'[38]

By the end of the decade, in conclusion, the Cuban Revolution faced an impasse. The economy was in a crisis, the Cubans were restless, and the regime was isolated internationally, increasingly reliant on Soviet support. A new road towards development and independence had to be constructed. Characteristically, Castro bent to the task, somewhat chastened by the failures of the sixties to judge by his speeches, but with the same will and pragmatism that he had displayed on numerous occasions in the past.

. . .

NOTES AND REFERENCES

1. Llerena M 1978 *The Unsuspected Revolution*. Ithaca, New York, Cornell University Press, p. 200
2. *Verde Olivo*, 5 March 1967
3. *Revolutción*, 20 Nov. 1959
4. Granma Weekly Review (*GWR*), 13 Dec. 1987
5. 'La Planificación Socialista, su Significado', in Guevara E 1967 *Obra Revolucionaria*. Ediciones Era, Mexico, 2nd ed., 1968, pp. 602–10
6. Domínguez J I 1978 *Cuba: Order and Revolution*. Harvard University, Cambridge, MA, pp. 174–8
7. Dumont R 1974 *Is Cuba Socialist?* Viking Press, New York, p. 57
8. *Nueva Industria*, 3 Oct. 1963; Brundenius C 1981 *Economic Growth, Basic Needs and Income Distribution in Revolutionary Cuba*, University of Lund, pp. 71–5
9. *Granma*, 12 Feb. 1985
10. Quoted in Brundenius 1981 p. 71
11. *Granma*, 27 July 1970
12. Op.cit., 27 July 1966

13. *Revolución*, 15 March 1965
14. Domínguez 1978 p. 161; Brundenius 1981 p. 78; Castro's speech of 1979, 'Vietnam is not alone', in Taber M (ed.) 1981 *Fidel Castro Speeches: Cuba's Internationalist Foreign Policy 1975–80*. Pathfinder, New York, p. 142
15. *Granma*, 27 July 1966
16. Op.cit., 13 Jan 1968
17. Castro R 1968 *Desenmascaran la microfacción*. Hoy, Minas (Uruguay)
18. Dumont 1974 pp. 41–7, 61–2, 71–95
19. *GWR*, 24 March 1968
20. Brundenius 1981 p. 79
21. Franqui C 1983 *Family Portrait with Fidel*. Jonathan Cape, London, p. 140
22. Author's conversation with Pablo Armando Fernández, Aug. 1968
23. See, e.g., *Verde Olivo*, 20 and 27 Oct. 1968
24. E.g., in the fourth Congress of UNEAC reported in *Cuba Socialista*, no. 32, March–April 1988
25. Teresa Casuso, quoted in Szulc T 1987 *Fidel: a Critical Portrait*. Hutchinson, London, p. 274
26. *Verde Olivo*, 6 Oct. 1968 p. 62
27. See Castro's introduction to Guevara E 1968 *El Diario del Che en Bolivia*. Instituto del Libro, Havana, pp. VII–VIII
28. Karol K S 1970 *Guerrillas in Power: the Course of the Cuban Revolution*. Hill & Wang, New York, p. 506
29. *GWR*, 25 Aug. 1968
30. E.g., Bourne P 1987 *Castro: a Biography of Fidel Castro*. Macmillan, London, p. 271; and to some extent Szulc 1987 pp. 504–5
31. *GWR*, 25 Aug. 1968
32. *Bohemia*, 13 June 1969
33. *GWR*, 26 Oct. 1969
34. Domínguez 1978 pp. 177–8
35. *Granma*, 27 July 1970
36. Domínguez 1978 pp. 275–6
37. *Granma*, 27 July 1970
38. *GWR*, 4 Jan. 1976

Chapter 6

THE REVOLUTIONARY GODFATHER

The abortive sugar harvest campaign of 1969–70 marked the end of a cycle of efforts by the Revolutionary regime to break out of the iron circle of underdevelopment and dependency by mobilising the Cuban people through ideological appeal. At the same time, the exaggerated hopes that the Revolution could be exported to Latin America were dashed towards the end of the decade by the destruction of most of the continent's guerrilla groups. From the beginning of the seventies, the Cuban leaders sought to redirect their foreign policy and reshape Cuba's economic and political structures to accommodate them to the new internal and external constraints. One of the most important of these was the increasing dependence on the Soviet Union, without whose aid and favourable terms of trade the Revolution simply could not survive. The deepening economic crisis facing Cuba after the campaign made the leadership all the more sensitive to Soviet pressure for internal reform and a re-alignment of its foreign policy.

The reforms that followed in the first half of the decade brought Cuba's economic and political institutions into line with those of the Soviet Union. With the co-operation of numerous Soviet advisers, Cuba's economic agencies and enterprises were restructured. A Soviet–Cuban Commission was set up in December 1970 to co-ordinate the use of Soviet aid, and two years later Cuba became a fully integrated member of the Soviet bloc common market, CMEA. A new system of economic management was gradually evolved in the seventies and was in operation by the end of the decade. It provided for a certain measure of financial accountability, profitability, and materials flow among enterprises, as well as the introduction of a wide range of material incentives. On the political front, a new constitution largely modelled on that of the Soviet Union was approved in a referendum in 1976. It established three pyramids of power, the Council of Ministers or government, the Communist Party headed by the Politburo, and the Organs of People's Power (OPP), an institutional innovation with no obvious parallel in the Soviet system, providing for elected assemblies on a municipal level and indirect suffrage on a provincial level leading to a National Assembly and a Council of State to which the Council of Ministers is accountable.

Some commentators have defined this process of institution-alisation as the 'Sovietisation' of Cuba, ascribing the changes to the influence of Moscow.[1] The Soviet Union under Brezhnev did indeed have several reasons for wishing to bring the island into its fold; Cuba would pose less of a threat to the process of *détente* with the United States and the cost of supporting the Cuban economy could be spread among other socialist bloc countries. The Kremlin was also in a position to insist on a reorganisation of Cuba's economic institutions as a price of any further underwriting of its economy.

Yet it could be argued that the institutional reforms were the result more of the internal dynamic of the Revolution than of Soviet pressure. Throughout the sixties, Cuba had been governed by a cabinet led by Castro, in which all legislative and executive powers were vested. The Cuban Communist Party, established in 1965, had not functioned as a mass party and indeed held its first congress only in 1976. Of the mass organisations, only the Committees for the Defence of the Revolution had grown any popular roots. The highly centralised system of government of the sixties corresponded, in the eyes of the Revolutionary leadership, to the urgent need to ensure the survival of the Revolution in the face of American hostility and to rouse Cuba's workers for the task of development while guaranteeing social equity. Castro and his closest followers saw themselves as the trustees of the Revolution acting on behalf of the Cuban people until they were ready to assume the responsibilities of self-government in a socialist society. As Che Guevara had written, 'Our aspiration is that the party become a mass one, but only when the masses reach the level of development of the vanguard, that is, when they are educated for communism.'[2]

By 1970, however, it was clear that this political model was not functioning well. The most obvious sign was the widespread absenteeism and the low levels of productivity registered in the summer and autumn. In elections to the Advanced Workers' Movement in the same period, many of the existing holders of the privileged status of exemplary worker were voted out in a tacit display of criticism of this Cuban version of Stakhanovism. The Revolutionary leadership was quick to respond to the growing crisis of confidence among Cuban workers. Castro held a twelve-hour debate with workers' representatives in Havana province in September, insisting on the presence of three of his top men, including the Minister of Labour. During the meeting the leaders were treated to a barrage of detailed complaints about the inefficiency of management at all levels. In tune with the new mood of self-criticism, Castro was not sparing in his attacks on excessive centralisation in economic planning, referring to the problem of 'diabolical centralisations'. He took Cuba's technocrats to task, describing them as 'Well-prepared but unrealistic people. That is, they have technological training, they have learnt a bit of mathematics, but they are very underdeveloped as far as the realities of life are concerned.'

However, his most significant criticism was directed against the whole model of accumulation through moral mobilisation that had dominated the policy of the Revolutionary leadership in the sixties. Using a typically military metaphor, he declared,

> we have to become conscious of the fact that in a time of crisis ... the Revolution ... has perhaps advanced too far. It is even perhaps like an army that penetrated too far into the enemy ranks, with troops that were not sufficiently well trained, with soldiers that were still insufficiently warrior-like, and with some very bad commanders. ... Perhaps our greatest illusion [idealismo] was to have believed that a society that has only just come out of its shell in a world that has been subjected for years to the law of the strongest ... could become, at a stroke, a society in which everyone behaved in an ethical and moral fashion.[3]

The process of institutional and economic reform in the seventies was intended in part to overcome the crisis in the labour movement that had arisen during the sugar campaign. In the sixties, labour had been viewed as an army, subject to a hierarchy of command. Now Castro was calling for its democratisation. In his concluding speech to the meeting of Havana province branch of the Confederation of Cuban Workers, he urged, 'The number one contribution of workers is to democratize themselves, to constitute a strong and powerful labour movement.'[4] The new tone was in sharp contrast to Castro's censoriousness towards workers' representatives during the first congress of the CTC after the Revolution on 18 November 1959. Reprimanding them for the 'shameless spectacle' they had presented when divisions between anti-Communist workers of the 26th July Movement and PSP representatives had risen to the surface, he had exclaimed,

> I had the impression that you were playing with a revolution you held in your hands; I had the sensation – a hard, disagreeable sensation – as of a mass of men, of leaders, in fact, who were not behaving in a responsible way . . . if, indeed, the working-class or its representatives know what they are doing. . . . We have said: the revolution demands that the workers be organized like an army.[5]

Castro's call for greater democracy in the labour movement, however, was not the expression of a new-found conviction about the virtues of pluralism. Rather, it arose from the urgent need to raise productivity and improve efficiency on the shop floor. Exhortations from the leadership to work harder were no longer enough; new mechanisms were needed to boost production. The labour unions had always been viewed by the leadership not as the defenders of workers' wages and conditions but, in Raúl Castro's words, 'as vehicles for orientation, directives and goals which the revolutionary power must convey to the working masses'.[6] In the late sixties, the CTC had not been encouraged to grow by the leadership and it had been the Advanced Workers' Movement that had received official publicity. As Castro disingenuously confessed to the crowds:

> for the last two years our workers' organizations had

taken a back seat – not through the fault of either the workers' organizations or the workers themselves but through our fault, the Party's fault, the fault of the country's political leadership. Was this done consciously? No! It happened somewhat unconsciously, spontaneously; it happened as a result of certain idealisms. And this way, in creating an organization which we believe is also important – the organization of the Advanced Workers' Movement – the workers' movement, in general, was neglected.[7]

After 1970, in contrast, CTC branches were set up in thousands of workplaces and delegate congressses began to be held regularly. The CTC itself was relaunched in November 1973 with a new structure and statutes. That the call for democracy was more to do with tightening labour discipline than giving rein to rank-and-file demands was borne out by the simultaneous campaign against absenteeism and 'loafing' launched by Castro. From the platform, he railed at the widespread slackness at work, turning his stern gaze at individual workplaces. Issue after issue of the official paper *Granma* in autumn 1970 contained slogans linking democratisation to the campaign against absenteeism, and in the following year an 'anti-loafing' law was passed providing for a range of sanctions against supposedly 'work-shy' people.

Bolstering the labour unions was also intended to enable a new system of work organisation to be introduced as part of the package of economic reforms. The new strategy represented a return to the more orthodox policies essayed briefly between 1963 and 1966. Higher productivity would come about, it was now believed, by offering material incentives to workers and establishing work norms.[8] Castro's call for greater democracy in the labour movement was designed partly to prepare workers for a more rigorous system of control over their work. Describing the round of discussions with workers' representatives in the autumn of 1970, he said: 'through a profound process of debate with the workers and through the participation of the masses in the search for solutions to our problems, an opportune mood had been created for the introduction of new schemes of organization and work norms'.[9]

The new emphasis on such things as work quotas, clocking-in, and material incentives represented a setback for those in the leadership, not least for Castro himself, who had believed they could infuse the labour movement with a new morality based on patriotic self-sacrifice. The compulsive drive for accumulation had to be slowed down because many workers were not responding to moral appeals. Although Castro calculated that only 20 per cent of workers were 'shirkers', the high rate of absenteeism and the low level of productivity at the turn of the decade suggested that dissatisfaction among workers was more widespread than he acknowledged publicly.[10] The new labour strategy, however, did not mean abandoning moral incentives altogether but finding a different balance between monetary and moral rewards. In a speech on 26 July 1973, Castro defined it thus:

> Together with moral incentive, we must also use material incentive,without abusing either one, because the former would lead us to idealism, while the latter would lead to individual selfishness. We must act in such a way that economic incentives will not become the exclusive motivation of man, nor moral incentives serve to have some live off the work of the rest.[11]

The reform of the unions was part of a wider restructuring of the political and economic system in Cuba in the seventies. Like the changes in work practices, the reforms were more a response to the failure of the campaigns of the late sixties and to the pressures from below that they generated than the result of Soviet pressure. Their interlocking objectives were to decentralise to some extent the administration of government and the management of the economy in order to make them more efficient, and to give the mass of Cubans a greater say in the running of local affairs so that criticism at the base could rise to the top. This was in contrast to the radical period of the late sixties when, in Castro's words, the idea had prevailed that 'critical comments and the denunciations of errors were playing into the hands of the enemy'.[12] Neither of these aims, however, was intended to lessen the political control of the Party and the Revolutionary leadership.

The three fundamental measures of this institutionalisation were the creation of the Organs of Popular Power (OPP),the new system of management (*Sistema de Dirección y Planificación de la Economía*, briefly described earlier) and the reorganisation of the top government posts. The creation of the OPP devolved many of the bureaucratic functions hitherto performed by the regional administrative bodies to locally elected assemblies at municipal and provincial levels. The new structure allowed a certain measure of democratic control over local affairs. It also represented for the leadership a more reliable system of consultation and assessment of public opinion than the informal procedures they had adopted throughout the sixties. At a higher level, however, the Communist Party had considerable control over the nomination of candidates to the provincial assemblies and the supreme body of the OPP, the National Assembly. In keeping with the elitist tradition of the Revolution, the higher echelons of the OPP were not intended to represent public opinion but to select the most active and reliable cadres.

The reorganisation of the government was also a reaction to the policy failures of the sixties. Until 1972, the most important government functions had been concentrated in the hands of a small cabinet consisting of Castro and a handful of leaders of the Revolution. Beneath them, government administration had also been highly centralised; planning and execution of policy had been dealt with centrally in Havana and decisions were passed down through a hierarchy of administration at different levels. Throughout the sixties, Castro had acted as the Revolution's troubleshooter, ombudsman, and animator. Wandering restlessly across Cuba, he had sorted out local problems, and launched a multitude of projects that often bypassed or even clashed with plans drawn up by the central Planning Board, Juceplan, and the ministries. The French agronomist René Dumont, who accompanied him on several of his trips around the island, observed later: 'Castro's personal ideas constitute another official programme at least as imperative as the first [that of the Planning Board and ministries]. Attempts are therefore made to do everything and what happens is that only a little of everything is done.' Castro's enormous prestige allied to his overriding self-confidence had made it difficult to contradict or reverse his frequent initiatives. Castro, Dumont continued, 'follows his own ideas, convinced that they are the best. Thus he assumes unchecked personal power and this fosters a courtier-like approach in those around him. When he throws his beret on the ground and flies into one of his rages everybody quakes and fears reprisals.'[13]

Although many of Castro's projects were successful, there were others that had negative consequences, diverting precious resources towards abortive experiments. His mostly costly initiative, as we have seen, had been the sugar campaign of 1969–70. The price that had to be paid for it was not just a dislocation of the economy but a fall in confidence among many Cubans about the direction of the Revolution. The 1970 crisis led to a restructuring of the government to ensure a more rational organisation of the economy. In 1972 the cabinet was enlarged to include an executive committee consisting of a new layer of deputy ministers charged with a range of responsibilities hitherto held by Castro and a handful of his ministers. Alongside the deputy ministers were the heads of the central organisations, such as Juceplan and the National Bank. Directly responsible to this newly enlarged cabinet were a number of state organisations of non-ministerial rank and beneath them were provincial and regional boards entrusted with co-ordinating and executing government decisions.[14] Cuba's administrative structures were further reorganised in 1976 to bring them into line with those of the Soviet bloc. As for Castro, although by 1976 he was Head of State, Party leader, President of the cabinet, and Commander-in-Chief of the armed forces, he gradually shed direct ministerial responsibilities as the decade progressed.

The administrative reforms thus allowed a greater degree of delegation and specialisation in the higher ranks of the government. The economy was thereby protected from the sometimes disruptive interventions of Castro. But they also helped to shield the President himself from the consequences of policy failures. The officially declared shift from individual to collective leadership helped to give the regime greater stability in the years following the trauma of the abortive sugar campaign. The change in emphasis was signalled by Castro's speech on 26 July 1973. Greatly underplaying his own role in the late sixties he declared, with reference to the foundation of the Communist Party in 1965,

We began to advance along the new path, without chieftains, without 'personalities', without factions, in

110

a country in which , historically, personality conflicts were the cause of great political defeats. . . . In the uncertain times of the 26th July and in the early years of the Revolution, individuals played a decisive role, a role now carried out by the Party. Men die, but the Party is immortal.[15]

The reorganisation of government may have put Castro at one remove from many centres of administrative decision-making, but his position at the head of the Revolution, now confirmed in the Constitution, was unquestioned. There is little proof to suggest that the failure of the sugar campaign seriously undermined his authority, as some commentators have argued.[16] Admittedly, it represented a defeat for his strategy of austerity and patriotic mobilisation, while it strengthened the voice of those calling for more orthodox policies who had been elbowed aside in the radical period of the late sixties. The return to prominence of notable pre-Revolutionary Communists such as Carlos Rafael Rodríguez, previously Minister Without Portfolio and now chair of the new Soviet–Cuban Commission and Deputy Prime Minister in 1972, indicated an important shift in the balance of interests among the leadership. In a sense, it was a new, more extreme version of the crisis of 1963 when the Revolutionary leadership had been obliged to abandon their drive to industrialise Cuba by forced march. But it would appear now that Castro, as in 1964, was able to regain the initiative by becoming the most eloquent advocate of the new policy. He was also able to recover his prestige through foreign policy initiatives, the most spectacular of which was the campaign in Angola (discussed in Chapter 7). There is no question that in the seventies Castro was still regarded with enormous affection and respect by most Cubans; as the supreme leader of the Revolution he was irreplaceable.

Power relations in the Cuban regime, however, are difficult to judge because the internal debates among the leadership are not available for consultation. As a result, any account of relations within the regime has to rely on inference. Some writers on post-1970 Cuba claim on this basis to have identified cleavages among the Revolutionary elite around political and economic tendencies.[17] Yet it is more reasonable to assume that, in contrast to the sixties when the ideological differences among the supporters of the Revolution had risen to the surface and had been hammered out, the Revolutionary leadership remained a relatively cohesive force in the seventies. For one thing, the economic base for the emergence of autonomous elites has not existed in Cuba. The new decentralising measures introduced in the seventies did not reduce the prerogative of the state as the centre of planning and resource allocation. For example, whereas enterprise managers were given greater powers of decision-making at the level of individual firms, they were still subject to the overall control of the state. Second, all posts of any authority in the Revolutionary institutions, from military officers to government administrators, were subject to the discipline of the Communist Party whose system of democratic centralism ensured that once party policy had been decided it had to be carried out by members regardless of their position in the debate leading to the decision. Moreover, the growth of functional divisions within the regime was limited to some extent by the overlapping roles played by the different institutions. The military, for example, traditionally a relatively independent force in Latin America, was in Cuba strongly represented in the single party of the state and was entrusted with wide-reaching civilian tasks, ranging from public works engineering to providing unskilled labour for cane-cutting.

In the mid-seventies, eighteen people belonging to the top institutions of the state could be described as the most important decision-makers in Cuba. Apart from Castro and his brother Raúl, they were made up of veterans of the rebel army, civilian members of the 26th July Movement, and ex-members of the PSP, some of whom had been dropped from prominent public office during the radical period of the late sixties. Though their political origins were not necessarily important in determining their positions of power, it was significant that the majority had been close collaborators of Castro since at least the beginning of the guerrilla campaign, suggesting that loyalty to the leader of the Revolution was still perceived as an important criterion of political merit. Of the full central committee members elected in the first Congress of the Party in 1976, almost a third were military men, over 28 per cent were Party officials, and just under 18 per cent were in the administration.[18] As Commander-in-Chief of the armed forces, First Secretary of the Party, and President of the Council of State and the Council of Ministers, Castro was owed allegiance by the military, Party, and government officials alike.

There is some limited evidence of political differences in the seventies among the leadership and within the central committee but these do not seem to have taken organisational forms in the same way as the pro-Soviet pre-Revolutionary Communist faction of the early sixties. One of the most important sources of tension was the balance between economic and socio-political factors in economic planning. The shift in emphasis after 1970 from social and political values to cost effectiveness in economic decision-making was bound to give rise to strains not only among the middle-ranking officials charged with carrying out policy but also within the leadership. Although the new line was sanctioned by Castro, he had been, with Guevara, the most vociferous exponent of the primacy of politics over economics. Indeed, he would intervene once again in the mid-eighties, as we shall see, to correct the balance which, in his opinion, had gone too far towards purely quantitative calculations.

For the time being, it was the adherents of a more technical approach to economic planning who spoke out in criticism of the policies of the sixties. Undoubtedly they included some of the pre-Revolutionary Communists who had frowned on Guevara's ideas in the sixties and had been excluded from positions of power. But there were also critics within the government. In a speech at Havana University in 1972 the President, Osvaldo Dorticós, launched into an attack on the economic planners of the sixties that could well have applied in part to Castro himself: 'during all these years,' he said,

one of the most devalued indicators in our economic planning has been that of costs. It is frequent, it has been frequent up to now ... to talk at most about having reached such and such a production figure, having accomplished such and such a percentage, or having surpassed the plan. But when you asked one of these officials, or almost all of them, what the costs were, at what cost, with what use of material, human, and financial resources, none of them knew the answer. And this indicated a high degree of irresponsibility ... as if cost was something of a metaphysical entity.[19]

113

Among the new technocrats associated with the policy change, there was a similar aversion to the methods of the sixties. The head of the Planning Board in 1979 declared, 'those comrades amongst us who have worked in the different state organisms . . . are impregnated with the old centralizing and in many cases bureaucratic habits and it is not always easy to shed these habits.'[20]

Another source of tension among the different interest groups within the regime was budget allocation; in this, the Cuban political system has been no different from most other forms of government. The military, in particular, has creamed off a large amount of Cuba's surplus (over 5 per cent of GNP during the seventies and eighties) indicating the importance of national defence since the Revolution and of military involvement abroad from the mid-seventies. But this also reflected the key role the military played in the Cuban economy. As the most powerful and professional elite in the regime, the military might have become the focus of a separate political tendency were it not for its close involvement in the economic and political life of Cuba. The top ranks of the military are not only members of the Communist Party subject to its discipline but are also participants in executing economic plans. Indeed, the dominant feature of the Revolutionary leadership has been the interlocking nature of their civic and military functions, best exemplified by the two Castro brothers. Nevertheless, the institutional reforms of the seventies gave rise to a greater functional separation within the Revolutionary establishment. The continued priority given to the military provoked the occasional complaints of civilian agencies. For example, when Cuba became involved in the war over Angolan independence in 1975, attempts were made by some enterprise managers to resist the compulsory enlistment of skilled workers to the military reserve. Their recalcitrance was made evident in a speech by Castro in which he said that it was necessary 'to combat the occasionally exaggerated criteria as to who cannot be dispensed with in production'.[21]

Yet for all the tensions that existed in the top echelons of the regime in the seventies, the Cuban leadership remained relatively united. The transition from the centralised and hierarchical model of the sixties to the more collective government of the mid-seventies onwards was achieved without bloodletting though not without disagreements. The broader structures of power created in the early seventies not only enabled the older generation of pre-Revolutionary Communists to return to positions of influence within the regime but also gave access to a new generation of administrators, technicians, officers, and party organisers. In fact, the more significant differences within the regime in recent years have tended to be generational, as we shall examine in Chapter 8. No radical changes of personnel took place in the top echelons of the party and the state during the seventies that might suggest any shift in the internal balance of power. Demotions occurred as a result of policy failures or supposed incompetence, while promotions tended to favour success, such as the appointment to the Council of State of two generals prominent in the Angolan operations of 1975.

Indeed, after the reforms of the early seventies, the leadership of the Revolution resembled something of an extended family whose inner nucleus was formed by the veterans of the *Granma* expedition and the Sierra campaign.[22] No longer directly responsible for all its activities, Fidel Castro now assumed the role of godfather to the Revolutionary family. Although he remained the ultimate source of authority and the arbiter of disputes, he was no longer in a position easily to impose policy against any branch of the family. The new constraints on his autonomy derived in part from the renewed influence of the Soviet Union. The integration of Cuba into Comecon and the massive military aid provided by Moscow combined to create strong institutional links between Cuban economic and military personnel and their East European counterparts. Consequently, although Castro had been able to act decisively against the pro-Soviet faction in 1962 and 1968, the cost of challenging top administrators close to Soviet officials became much higher in the seventies.[23]

The new institutional framework also made it more difficult for Castro to intervene in areas of responsibility that had been devolved to lower levels of administration. In the mid-sixties, he had launched an anti-bureaucratic drive, declaring, 'the future progress of the Revolution will be measured by the fall each year in the number of administrative employees . . . and by the rise in the number of metal-workers each year in our country'. In the seventies, on the contrary, he was calling for the strengthening of the state apparatus on the grounds

that the excessive weight of the Party in the previous decade
had led to inefficiency.[24] As political control over economic
agencies receded, the top personnel of the ministries were
given greater latitude to run their own affairs within the
framework of national planning. Moreover, the new economic
organisation espoused by the regime did not require Castro to
act any longer as guide and model. He no longer appeared at
every opportunity to launch a fresh scheme or explain a new
policy, to berate and inspire the Cubans. The shift in Castro's
role was expressed in his changing appearance. The image of
the young athletic man in battle fatigues with a cigar clenched
between his teeth tearing about the countryside in a jeep gave
way, as the seventies progressed, to that of a dignified rather
portly statesman in bemedalled army uniform, his beard going
grey, presiding over ceremonies for foreign heads of state.

No simple picture, therefore, can be drawn of the structure
of power in Cuba in the seventies. Castro did not pull all the
strings, as some Western commentators have argued, but
nor was his power confined purely to the functions assigned
to him by the Constitution, as official Cuban statements
assert. The institutional reforms enshrined his authority as
supreme leader but it created new centres of power that
Castro could not ignore. Internal policy was thus shaped
by a complex interaction between the various branches of
the Revolutionary family. It was also strongly influenced
by pressures outside the immediate family circle. Not least
among these was public opinion, expressed informally or
through the mass organisations of the Revolution; indeed, it
had been the workers' declining enthusiasm for productivity
goals that had hastened the reorganisation of the political
system in Cuba. Other powerful pressures from outside
were the political and economic constraints that accompanied
Cuba's increasing integration with the Soviet bloc. Castro no
longer enjoyed the virtually unlimited autonomy to define
policy that he had had in the sixties. It is likely that the
policies which he formulated as Head of State were the
result more of a consensus within the highest ranks of the
regime than of the imposition of his own authority. Yet he
continued to wield enormous influence on these decisions.
In any disagreement, the balance of power was tilted in his
direction because he could call on an immense power outside
the debating chamber. Castro's ability to override opinions

that contradicted his own was at its most limited in the early seventies. Only when some of these policies faltered, as in the mid-eighties, would he seize the opportunity once again to redirect the course of the Revolution personally. By his own admission, Castro played little part in the process of institutional reforms. That he was not entirely happy with the way it was done was revealed many years later in an interview with an Italian journalist. Referring to the change in policy from the radicalism of the late sixties to the orthodoxy of the early seventies, he confessed, 'We had gone through a period of self-sufficiency during which we believed we knew more than other people and could do things better than them, and we moved on to another phase, in which I was not personally involved, in which a tendency developed to copy. I believed we copied bad things well and good things badly.'[25] Instead, Castro's energies in the seventies were consumed in foreign policy. This was not because he was bored by the drab scene confronting him in Cuba, as Tad Szulc suggests in his biography of Castro.[26] Nor was it merely because the new division of labour within the Cuban government released him from an immediate commitment to the running of the economy. His intense involvement in external relations in the seventies was the direct result of a shift in Cuba's foreign strategy that accompanied the transformation of internal policy. And in his foreign as in his domestic policies, Castro showed once again his talent for making the best of the opportunities that came his way to raise his own standing and that of the Revolution.

. . .

NOTES AND REFERENCES

1. E.g., Mesa-Lago C 1974 *Cuba in the 1970s. Pragmatism and Institutionalization.* University of New Mexico; also Domínguez J I 1978 *Cuba: Order and Revolution.* Harvard University, Cambridge, MA
2. Guevara E 1967 *Man and Socialism in Cuba.* Book Institute, Havana.
3. *Granma*, 8 Sept. 1970
4. Op. cit., 10 Sept. 1970
5. Quoted in Franqui C 1983 *Family Portrait with Fidel.* Jonathan Cape, London, pp. 230–2

6. *Granma weekly Review (GWR)* 26 Sept. 1974
7. Op. cit., 4 Oct. 1970
8. Pérez H 1979 *Sobre las dificultades objetivas de la revolución. Lo que el pueblo debe saber. Política*, Havana
9. *Granma*, 25 Jan. 1971
10. Op. cit., 8 Sept. 1970
11. *GWR*, 5 Aug. 1973
12. Minà G 1988 *Il racconto di Fidel*. Mondadori, Milan, pp. 153–4
13. Dumont R 1974 pp. 107 and 111
14. *Granma*, 25 Nov. 1972
15. *GWR*, 5 Aug. 1973
16. E.g., Mesa-Lago 1978 and González E 'Institutionalization, Political Elites and Foreign Policies', in Blasier C and Mesa-Lago C (eds) 1979 *Cuba in the World*. University of Pittsburgh, pp. 3–36
17. Mesa-Lago 1974; González 1979; Domínguez 1978. For a critique of these various accounts of power in post-1970 Cuba, see Zimbalist A (ed.) 1988 *Cuban Political Economy: Controversies in Cubanology*. Westview, Boulder, Co, and London
18. Domínguez 1978 pp. 307–15
19. *Economía y Desarrollo*, May–June 1972 pp. 30–1
20. Pérez 1979
21. *GWR*, 4 Jan. 1976, quoted in Domínguez 1978 p. 355
22. The simile has been used in González E 'Political Succession in Cuba', in *Studies in Comparative Communism*, 9 (1 and 2), Spring-Summer 1976, pp. 80–107, but much of his speculation about tendencies within the leadership is questionable: see Bengelsdorf C 'Cubanology and Crises: the Mainstream looks at Institutionalization', in Zimbalist (ed.) 1988 pp. 212–25
23. Domínguez 1978 p. 382
24. *Verde Olivo*, 5 March 1967, and *GWR* 4 Jan. 1976
25. Minà 1988 p. 142
26. 'He refused to settle for any kind of status quo, and in the second half of 1970 turned away from the depressing domestic scene and its economic problems, to international problems and controversies on which he thrived.' Szulc T 1987 *Fidel: a Critical Portrait*. Hutchinson, London, p. 511

Chapter 7

THE WORLD STATESMAN

Towards the end of the sixties, Cuba had stood virtually alone in the world, harassed by the United States, ostracised by most Latin American countries, and increasingly frowned on by the Soviet Union. Ten years later, on the contrary, the island enjoyed an international prestige out of all proportion to its size and economic strength. Cuba was chosen as the host country for the Sixth Conference of the Non-Aligned Movement in 1979, with Castro as chairman for a four-year period. Thirty-five countries were receiving military and civil aid from Cuba, and like an elder statesman, Castro was giving advice to new revolutionary regimes in different parts of the world.

Cuba's new international influence derived in part from the transformation of the Third World's standing in the seventies. Three events in particular contributed to this change in the balance of power: the oil crisis, the Vietnam War, and the fall of the Portuguese empire in Africa. The cartel of mainly Third World oil-producing nations took advantage of the growing reliance of industrialised economies on oil to push up the price of crude in 1973, provoking the first major crisis in Western capitalism since the Second World War. The defeat of the United States at the hands of the Vietcong and North Vietnam represented an important psychological boost to the cause of Third World nationalism. The threat of American intervention overseas thereby receded; apart from the Vietnamese and the Cambodians, the Cubans were the ones to benefit most, having felt the marines breathing down their necks for a decade. Third, the 1974 military coup in Portugal led to the dismantling in Africa of the last of the old European colonies and the rise of three new nations.

The mood of self-confidence now prevailing in the South encouraged the Cuban leadership to play a new assertive role in world affairs. As David to the American Goliath, Cuba commanded respect in much of the Third World.

The ability of the Cuban regime to influence international events was due in great measure to the Soviet connection. The return of Cuba to the fold of loyal allies of Moscow after 1968 renewed the flow of oil and capital goods from the Eastern bloc as well as military aid and training. It also opened many diplomatic doors. Impelled by a more pragmatic foreign policy than in the sixties, the Cuban leaders found new allies in the Third World who looked to the Revolution for inspiration and welcomed its foreign aid. But Cuba's intense involvement overseas flowed above all from the immense energies released by the Revolution. Thousands of volunteers poured out of the island on medical, educational, technical, and military missions abroad. This diversion of scarce domestic resources towards foreign aid can only be explained by the overwhelming support of the Cuban people for the internationalist aims proclaimed by the Revolution.

The diplomatic successes of Cuba in the seventies also owed much to Castro. Freed from the direct management of domestic affairs by the reorganisation of the government, he plunged into an intense schedule of state visits abroad and talks with visiting heads of state in Cuba itself. Before he set off in 1972 on a two-month tour of ten countries in Africa and Eastern Europe, he declared his confidence in the new structure of leadership:

> Only a few years ago, none of us would even dream of being outside our country for too long, considering the way the imperialists were acting, with their threats and all the rest of it. Somebody always had to be around. Fortunately, things are different now. Despite the imperialists, their threats and their problems, we know that we have a staunch people, a firm Revolution, and a sound leadership made up of men who are more than capable of carrying through any task and facing any situation.[1]

Castro's visits were not merely ceremonial events but often served to initiate or build closer economic and military ties with allies abroad. While he conducted top-level talks, more concrete bilateral negotiations were dealt with by the next layer of Cuba's leaders – the President, Osvaldo Dorticós, Fidel's brother, Raúl Castro, the Minister of the Armed Forces and the much-respected senior politician and pre-Revolutionary Communist, Carlos Rafael Rodríguez, who was in charge of economic and diplomatic foreign relations. Beneath these lay the ministries and alongside them the powerful planning and military commissions linking Cuba and the Soviet bloc.

Although he had to work within these institutional constraints, Castro enjoyed more autonomy in the formulation of foreign policy than in domestic affairs, not merely because he was directly responsible for external relations as Head of State but also because he had always been the most decided advocate of the Revolution's international vocation. Although all policy was presented as the fruit of collective decision, a number of typically Castroist features can be identified in Cuba's foreign policy which suggest that he exercised a decisive influence over its development. The most important of these was the stress on international solidarity. The primacy of policies over economics has been one of Castro's enduring principles in domestic affairs; the same ideological component can be found in Cuban foreign policy in the seventies and eighties. Puzzled by the apparent absence of self-interest in much of Cuba's international involvement, some commentators have seen it as an expensive idiosyncrasy; others explain it away by arguing that Cuba was merely acting as the Soviet Union's surrogate abroad.[2] Castro himself claimed that Cuban foreign policy was motivated by the highest principles. In a conversation with foreign correspondents in 1983, he declared,

> we are not very nationalistic; we are patriots . . . and we are resolutely faithful to our political principles. Many times we have known how to sacrifice our national interests for the sake of the principles of our revolution and our internationalist principles. North Americans do not understand that, it puzzles them . . . our homeland is not just Cuba; our homeland is also humanity. We are learning to think in terms of humanity.[3]

Yet it can be argued that Castro's foreign policy responded to a more concrete objective than human solidarity and a more nationalistic role than that of the Soviet Union's agent abroad. In the sixties, he had sought unsuccessfully to consolidate the Revolution by spreading it abroad and creating a solid economy at home. His foreign policy in the seventies, on the other hand, was the pursuit of independence by mainly diplomatic means. Castro's long-term strategy was to forge unity between Third World countries, in particular in Latin America, in order to alter the unfavourable terms of trade between developed and underdeveloped nations. In numerous speeches and interviews, he suggested that the fundamental division in the world was between the underdeveloped South and the industrialised North.[4] Like the Maoists he saw the world as a collection of competing nations organised politically into blocs but separated by a more important division between rich and poor countries, or capitalist and proletarian nations. Although solidarity towards the exploited of all lands was repeatedly stressed, it was nation or people rather than class that defined policy. From this perspective, anti-imperialism was more important than anti-capitalism, and the attitude adopted towards the United States defined friend or foe. Hence Castro supported the Dergue, the pro-Soviet military regime in Ethiopia, and later defended General Noriega of Panama and the Argentine military junta during the Malvinas or Falklands War.[5]

Castro's diplomatic ventures served a dual purpose: to raise Cuba's standing in the world but also to consolidate the regime at home. His renewed popularity in Cuba in the seventies, after the crisis of 1969–70, owed a lot to his ostentatious display of world statesmanship. He continued to be admired as the man who restored national pride by taking on the United States; now, increasingly, he was also seen as an international statesman who was giving Cuba a new standing in the world community. It was a diplomatic circus to compensate for the lack of bread. Much prominence was given to his travels abroad and to the state visits of Third World leaders who came in growing numbers to Cuba. Castro's expansive gestures, embracing foreign statesmen, berating Cuba's enemies on international platforms, and giving lengthy interviews to a stream of fascinated foreign correspondents and politicians, were meant as much for domestic as for international consumption.

Cuba's new foreign policy in the seventies was the result not of Soviet pressure so much as a re-evaluation in the light of changing circumstances abroad. Three objectives may be singled out. First, Castro and the Cuban leaders continued to seek new alliances in the Third World through military missions and foreign aid programmes whose dual purpose was to end Cuba's isolation in the international community and lessen its dependence on the Soviet Union. At the same time, they aimed to increase their leverage over the Soviet Union by becoming its indispensable ally in the Third World. By doing so, they hoped to give themselves greater autonomy in the formulation of domestic and foreign policy while ensuring the continued economic support of the Soviet Union. Third, they made repeated attempts to open a dialogue with Washington in order to ease the pressure of the siege that the United States continued to impose on Cuba. These three objectives were not always compatible, and throughout the seventies Castro's consummate skill as a politician was employed to squeeze the maximum advantage out of Cuba's foreign involvement without undermining them.

Although Cuban foreign policy in the sixties had taken its own revolutionary experience as a model for Latin America, the new strategy recognised that there were different paths towards national emancipation depending on local circumstances. Castro's pronouncements in the two Declarations of Havana in the early sixties had acknowledged that both the military and the Catholic Church could play a progressive role in the struggle for national assertion and reform in Latin America. The rise on the continent of a reformist current in the armed forces, exemplified by the military regime in Peru, and the emergence of a new movement in the Latin American Church placing stress on the struggle for social justice, strengthened the belief that change would come about through an alliance of different social forces and no longer principally through guerrilla action. Moreover, the victory of the Popular Front in Chile under Salvador Allende seemed to vindicate the parliamentary road to socialism propounded by the Soviet Union and the orthodox Communist parties. Castro's own experience in the early fifties had led him to the opposite conclusion, that only armed action could bring about radical change. The history of Cuba suggested that the electoral process could too easily be perverted by corruption or destroyed by the military. Yet he was now cautiously acknowledging that in certain circumstances elections could be the centrepiece of a revolutionary strategy.

Castro articulated his new position during his three-week trip to Chile in November 1971. It was his first visit abroad for several years and it was a triumph. Received with open arms by the new President Allende and greeted everywhere by enthusiastic crowds, he toured the length of the narrow land, addressing students, copper and coal miners, nitrate workers, farm labourers, and immense audiences gathered in stadiums. With his characteristic blend of didacticism and concreteness he expounded his views on a multiplicity of themes, displaying his extraordinary ability to remember technical details and to marshal statistics. He was asked repeatedly if he supported the Chilean path to socialism considering that it contradicted the Cuban experience. 'Not only did we find no contradiction,' he said in answer to a question from a trade-union leader,

> but we also had seen a possibility concerning the concrete and real conditions that existed at the time of the elections [in Chile]. And this is the way we will always look with satisfaction on every new variation that may appear. And let every variation in the world make its appearance! If all roads lead to Rome, we can only wish for thousands of roads to lead to Revolutionary Rome![6]

Yet Castro was still not convinced about the possibility of a peaceful road to socialism. Nor had he lost his instinctive grasp of the relations of power. While he praised Allende's victory, he implicitly criticised the Chilean President's failure to mobilise the masses against the growing menace of the Right. Reacting to a US official who had recently expressed confidence that the Chilean government would not last long he said, 'such confidence is based on the weakness of the very revolutionary process, on weaknesses in the ideological battle, on weaknesses in the mass struggle, on weakness in the face of the enemy'.[7] Almost two years after his visit, on the eve of the September 1973 military coup, he wrote to Allende urging him to use the organised strength of the working class to halt the impending coup. Two weeks after the military had seized power, he declared in a mass rally in Cuba, 'The Chilean example teaches us the lesson that it is impossible to make the revolution with the people alone: arms are also necessary! And that arms alone aren't enough to make a revolution: people are also necessary.'[8]

He was not advocating social revolution, however. In his words to Chilean workers he continually stressed that they should subordinate their demands to the 'national interest'. Indeed, he implied that any battle they waged to improve their conditions would be a diversion from the war against imperialism.

I repeat that, in all seriousness, whether in Cuba or in Vietnam or in any country in Latin America, imperialism had been, is and will continue to be the principal enemy. Therefore, revolutionary strategy – and there's no question about this – must make tactics subordinate to the attainment of that fundamental objective, which is the liberation of our peoples of Latin America from imperialist domination.

In other words, the struggle for the rights of workers or any other section of society was not part of the struggle against imperialism and indeed could undermine it. Thus Castro reminded the copper workers of the damage they could do to the Chilean economy by coming out on strike. Instead, he advocated the broadest possible alliance of classes, from workers to the 'progressive sectors of the national bourgeoisie', to combat US imperialism. The inherent contradiction in his argument was that in practice social and political struggles could not be separated; to dampen workers' struggles was also to demobilise the most powerful obstacle against a military coup. Moreover, it was a typical section of the petty bourgeoisie, the Chilean lorry-owners, who provoked the crisis that led to the military take-over in 1973.

Castro's stress on the importance of national unity in Chile revealed that beneath his profession of proletarian internationalism lay a more powerful undercurrent of Pan-American nationalism that drew its inspiration from Bolívar and Martí. This vision assumed an underlying unity between all sections of society in Latin America except the most reactionary and oligarchic forces who, he argued, would not survive without the support of imperialism.

For America to be united and become Our America, the America Martí spoke of, it will be necessary to eradicate the very last vestige of those reactionaries who want the peoples to be weak so they can hold them in oppression and in subjection to foreign monopolies.

During his tour, Castro painted a picture of a free and united Latin America that would organise the exchange of commodities on a rational, co-operative basis. As usual, his illustrations of broad political ideas were vivid and calculated to relate to the immediate experience of his listeners. Speaking to workers of the nitrate mines in northern Chile, he explained how, because of the trade sanctions imposed against Cuba, Chile had had to invest large sums of money to produce beet sugar while Cuba had had to invest tens of millions of dollars in order to buy and produce nitrogen fertiliser, the end-product of the mineral the miners dug out of the mountain. From examples such as these, Castro drew an alluring picture of a Latin American common market, 'a union of sister nations that may become a large and powerful community in the world of tomorrow'.[9]

The renewal of hemispheric nationalism in many parts of Latin America and the Caribbean in the mid-seventies in the wake of the OPEC action seemed to corroborate Castro's words. The Cuban regime's moderation towards Latin America was in part a reflection of this new reality; the new policy also opened many diplomatic doors. Having been isolated in the late sixties, Cuba began to be accepted once more into the community of Latin American nations. From 1972, Cuba began to re-establish contacts with Latin American and Caribbean countries and shortly afterwards joined several regional development organisations. In 1975 the Latin American Economic System (SELA) was set up by twenty-five countries including Cuba in an attempt to co-ordinate economic policy and reduce their dependence on the United States. Three months previously, the Caribbean Committee of Development and Co-operation had been established in Havana after reciprocal state visits between Castro and the prime ministers of Jamaica, Guyana, and Trinidad-Tobago. In the same year, the Organisation of American States (OAS) voted to lift its sanctions against Cuba, though Castro had made clear that the island would never join the US-dominated organisation.

As the most decided opponent of US hegemony in Latin America, Castro welcomed the new initiatives. In the new multilateral organisations, Cuba could help to wean its fellow nations from the influence of the United States, as well as provide a bridge between Latin America and the Soviet bloc. In fact, the advantages for Cuba of membership in these hemispheric bodies were more political than economic. Castro's hopes for the emergence of a new economic bloc in Latin America underestimated the fact that the markets for Cuban products and the advanced technology necessary for the island's development were concentrated in the West, and in particular in Cuba's arch-enemy, the United States. Moreover, Latin American countries shared on the whole a similar pattern of economic activity centred on the production and processing of raw materials and the manufacture of consumer goods, with the result that their economies were more competitive than complementary.[10] For the time being, Cuba continued to depend on the Soviet Union for energy supplies and technology. If the island were to realise its economic potential, however, a fundamental transformation of US–Cuban relations would have to take place. The United States held the key to Cuba's development; it could provide the goods, the credits, the technology, and the tourist trade that Cuba so badly needed.

Yet Washington continued to regard the Cuban regime as a risk to US security and foreign policy goals, out of all proportion to Castro's real capacity to influence international events. US policy towards Cuba was still shaped partly by a gut reaction to the traumatic events of 1959–62. But it was also based on the belief that Castroism represented a threat to its major objective of encouraging the spread of Western capital to the Third World. Though there was some pressure within business circles in the United States to normalise relations with Cuba, Washington continued to insist on major concessions in internal and external policy on the part of the Cuban regime as a price of *détente* between the two countries.[11]

The necessity for a *rapprochement* with the United States was a bitter pill for Castro but one he had always been prepared to swallow. It may well have been urged on him at this time by the Soviet Union as part of its search for East–West *détente*; pressure may also have been exerted by the more pragmatic tendencies within the economic agencies of the Cuban government. Moreover, the US siege represented a continuous source of anxiety for Cubans; there were numerous flash-points such as the air and maritime hijackings on both sides and the occasional seizure of Cuban fishing vessels by US gunboats. The thaw in US–Cuban relations began indeed with an anti-hijacking agreement signed in 1973 with the Ford administration and continued with secret talks in the following year. In 1975, the United States joined with the majority of the OAS states in voting to end sanctions against Cuba.

However, Castro was not prepared to allow *détente* with the United States to detract from his objective of alliance-building in the Third World. When the Popular Movement for the Liberation of Angola appealed to Cuba for military aid in 1975 after a South African incursion in support of right-wing guerrillas threatened to disrupt their assumption of power on independence day, the Cuban leaders responded immediately by dispatching 1,000 troops to help defend the capital, Luanda. It was not a move calculated to appeal to the United States, and when in addition Cuba sponsored a conference in Havana in support of Puerto Rican independence, the *rapprochement* ground to a halt.

The gains that flowed from Cuba's intervention in the Angolan civil war far outweighed the losses following the breakdown of talks with the United States. The conflict in Angola had arisen on the eve of the country's independence from Portugal. The three guerrilla movements that had fought against the Portuguese had signed an agreement in Alvor in January 1975 calling for a provisional tripartite government and the celebration of elections in the same year. It was generally recognised that the MPLA, a left-wing nationalist movement loosely aligned with the Soviet Union and by far the most popular of the three organisations in Angola, would win a large majority of the votes. Its rivals, however, backed by covert CIA aid and South African, Zaïrean and mercenary troops, broke the agreement and launched a two-pronged military offensive on the MPLA, who controlled the capital. In August, South African troops crossed into Angola and in October, on the eve of independence day, launched an all-out drive on Luanda. The rapid Cuban air- and sea-lift that followed the MPLA's direct request to Castro helped to hold the capital for the MPLA. More than 20,000 Cuban troops crossed the Atlantic during the crisis; the flow of arms and soldiers was so great that Cuba itself was left exposed. By the end of November, the South African troops and the two rival guerrilla organisations were on the retreat, and four months later the MPLA were in full control of most of the newly independent Angola.

Most accounts agree that the Cuban decision to send troops to Angola was taken without consulting the Soviet Union. The Cubans had had close contact with the MPLA ever since Che Guevara had trained Congolese guerrillas in 1965. After MPLA leaders had attended the Tricontinental Conference in Havana in the following year, some of their guerrillas had received military training in Cuba. Castro and the Cuban leadership strongly identified with the struggle in Angola on several other accounts. Although Cuba was a Latin American nation, it also possessed deep cultural and racial roots in Africa through the Cuban descendants of African slaves. The MPLA was a movement in the mould of the Cuban regime, favouring state control of the economy and political centralisation. Cuba's military aid to the MPLA, moreover, increased its prestige among non-aligned nations, raising the hope that it could exert an even greater influence in the Third World. It was no coincidence that, less than four years later, Havana would be the venue of the Sixth Conference of the Non-Aligned Movement and Castro its new chairman.

The rewards of Cuban intervention were even greater on a domestic level. Though the intervention caused inevitable strains as the human cost of military involvement rose, the victory in Angola was a reaffirmation of the strength of the Revolution for many Cubans and a welcome source of national pride after the reverses of the late sixties and early seventies. Though he did not control military operations, Castro played a prominent role in the war as a military adviser and overall Commander-in-Chief of the Armed Forces. According to his friend, the Colombian writer Gabriel García Márquez, Castro

saw off all the ships, and before each departure he gave a pep talk to the soldiers. He personally had picked up the commanders of the battalion of special forces that left in the first flight and had driven them himself in his Soviet jeep to the foot of the plane ramp. There was no spot on the map of Angola that he couldn't identify or a physical feature that he hadn't memorised. His concentration on the war was so intense and meticulous that he could quote any figure on

Angola as if it were Cuba, and he spoke of Angolan cities, customs, and people as if he had lived there his entire life.

In the early part of the operation, García Márquez recalls,

> Castro remained up to fourteen hours straight in the operations room of the general staff, at times without eating or sleeping, as if he were in the battlefield himself. He followed the details of every battle with coloured pins on the detailed maps which covered the walls, and remained in constant communication with the top commands of the MPLA in a battlefield with a six-hour difference.[12]

Cuba's military intervention in Angola also must have raised the value of Havana in the Kremlin's calculations. After the adventurism of the Khrushchev years, the Soviet Union had been carrying out a cautious process of *détente* with the United States under the Brezhnev leadership. Its pursuit of *rapprochement* with the West, however, was at cross-purposes with Castro's long-term policy of reshaping relations between the North and South. For the Soviets, Third World politics were important only to the extent that they affected the balance of power between the United States and the socialist bloc. For Castro, though he intoned the ritual of Soviet doctrine, the key issue of world politics was the problem of underdevelopment and imperialism. Underlying their difference in strategy lay a deeper, unspoken division about the nature of revolutionary change. Soviet orthodoxy continued to maintain that the world-wide triumph of socialism was inevitable because the internal contradictions of capitalism would lead to its collapse. The strategy of peaceful coexistence was seen not as a disavowal of the struggle between the two systems but as a prerequisite of the eventual victory of socialism. Castro, on the contrary, continually laid stress on the importance of subjective conditions in the creation of a revolutionary situation. Indeed, the Cuban Revolution could only be explained in these terms; hence the strategy in the sixties of exporting the Cuban model to Latin America. Moreover, *détente* between East and West threatened to leave the South out in the cold. It is hard not to suspect that Castro's accommodation in the seventies to the Soviet doctrine of peaceful coexistence was against his better judgement. His words to Brezhnev in July 1972 had a hollow ring to them:

We fully agree with you, Comrade Brezhnev, when you say that the principle of peaceful co-existence and the successes obtained in this field can by no means lead to a weakening of the ideological struggle, which will increase and become more acute in the confrontation of the two systems.[13]

Nevertheless, events in Africa from the mid-seventies encouraged the Soviet leaders to become more involved in that continent even at the risk of provoking the United States. In this renewal of intervention abroad, the interests of Cuba and the Soviet Union converged. Cuba's credentials as an anti-imperialist Third World country were useful to the Soviet Union, while the Cuban leaders, by their material support for Soviet policies in Africa, were able to gain leverage over Moscow. Far from acting as the Kremlin's surrogate abroad, however, the Cuban leaders were able to pursue an independent foreign policy so long as it did not clash with that of the Soviet Union. The Angolan connection, for example, was not a high priority for the Kremlin, and the evidence suggests that it was Cuba, and Castro in particular, who took the initiative and encouraged greater Soviet involvement.[14]

Cuba's participation in the 1977–8 war between Ethiopia and Somalia, on the other hand, responded more to Soviet than Cuban interests. The Horn of Africa represented an area of great geo-strategic value for the USSR. As an ally of the Somali military regime for several years, the Soviet Union had had a naval base at Berbera on the Gulf of Aden. Events in the Horn of Africa in the mid-seventies precipitated a dramatic turn-about of international alliances in the area. In 1974 the US-backed regime of the Emperor Haile Selassie in neighbouring Ethiopia was overthrown by a military coup. The new junta that replaced the old regime, the Dergue, was itself taken over by radical officers three years later. The United States responded by cutting off its aid to Ethiopia, to which the Dergue replied by turning to the Soviet Union for arms. In its turn, the Somali regime, which had a long-standing dispute with Ethiopia over Somali claims to the Ogaden desert in the south, switched its allegiance to the United States. The change in partners also affected the civil war in Ethiopia between the government and the Eritrean Liberation Front. Having previously supported the territorial integrity of Ethiopia, the United States now backed the Eritrean independence movement.

The Soviet Union had sought to reconcile both sides in an effort to maintain its new influence in the region. In March 1977, acting almost certainly with the blessing of Moscow, Castro visited both the Ethiopian and Somali leaders to seek a settlement.[15] In June, however, the Somali forces, newly armed by the United States, invaded the Ogaden desert. In a move to legitimise its growing military support for Ethiopia, the Kremlin asked for Cuban troops to be involved in the campaign to push the Somali army out of the Ogaden. Strengthened by 15,000 Cuban soldiers and massive Soviet arms shipments, the Ethiopian forces launched a counter-offensive and by February 1978 had driven the Somali army back across the frontier.

Castro had originally supported Somali claims against Ethiopia. The radical shift in the Ethiopian regime in 1977, which brought to power a socialist-aligned junta, presented him with a dilemma. The subsequent about-turn in his policy towards the Horn of Africa could be justified on the grounds that Somalia had transgressed international law by invading the Ogaden. However, it was more difficult to explain away Cuba's alignment with a regime that was conducting a war of attrition against an oppressed national minority in Ethiopia, the Eritreans, who should have and indeed had once commanded Castro's support. Whereas the Soviet Union had an obvious interest in maintaining the territorial integrity of Ethiopia against secessionist claims because Eritrea commanded a strategic stretch of the Red Sea coast, Cuba had only Soviet goodwill to gain from its military involvement in Ethiopia. Castro attempted to resolve the contradiction by ensuring that Cuban troops were not engaged in the war against the Eritrean Liberation Front and by calling for a semi-autonomous status for Eritrea within Ethiopia. Nevertheless, his support for the Ethiopian military junta could not fail to mar his reputation among some Third World nations.

The price that Cuba was forced to pay for its international alignment with the Soviet Union was at its highest with the Soviet intervention in Afghanistan in December 1979. The invasion could not have come at a worse moment for Castro. The year 1979 had represented a climax in his career as a world statesman. In March, a coup in the neighbouring island of Grenada had brought to power a close ally of his, the popular Maurice Bishop, and in July the old dictator of Nicaragua, Anastasio Somoza, had been overthrown by an insurrection led by the Havana-aligned liberation movement, the Sandinistas. In September, Castro had risen before the representatives of ninety-four countries and liberation movements that formed the Non-Aligned Movement to make the keynote speech as chairman and host of its sixth conference in Havana. In all these events, Castro was able to demonstrate the new moderation of Cuba's foreign policy. As a kind of elder revolutionary statesman to the new Nicaraguan regime, he enjoined on the Sandinistas to be realistic in their policies. They needed to reconstruct the war-devastated economy of Nicaragua with the co-operation of all sectors of society, which meant, Castro implied, maintaining a mixed economy and a pluralist political system. In addition, he urged them to keep up good relations with the United States.[16]

Castro's speech at the conference of the Non-Aligned Movement had also been notable for the tone of conciliation it had adopted towards member countries with which Cuba had differences. Since the 1973 conference in Algiers, Castro had been the main spokesman of the thesis that the Soviet bloc was the natural ally of the Third World against Western imperialism, as against the argument put forward by China, among others, that the Soviet Union and the United States were both imperialist powers. Conscious that he could not carry many of the member countries with him at the conference, Castro had no longer insisted on Soviet alignment but instead had gone out of his way to reassure the assembly that Cuba would respect the different views represented there. 'We have many close friends at this conference,' he had declared, 'but we don't always agree with the best of them . . . . We will work with all member countries – without exception – to achieve our aims and to implement the agreements that are adopted. We will be patient, prudent, flexible, calm. Cuba will observe these norms throughout the years in which it presides over the movement.'[17]

Cuba's official support for Soviet intervention in Afghanistan, barely three months after the conference, deeply undermined Castro's claim to the moral leadership of the Third World. He was faced by a dilemma. Afghanistan had been a founder member of the Non-Aligned Movement, and for Cuba to sanction the massive intervention of Soviet troops in what was clearly a civil war was to make a nonsense of its non-aligned status, especially when it had the role of head of the Movement. At the same time, Cuba could not oppose the Soviet action without endangering its relationship with Moscow. When the Non-Aligned Movement came to vote on a UN resolution condemning the intervention, Cuba was among the nine nations that backed the Soviet Union against fifty-six that supported the resolution. Despite Cuban efforts to tone down support for the invasion, Castro's standing in the Third World was shaken.[18]

For Castro the Afghan events of 1979 must have evoked the ghost of the 1968 invasion of Czechoslovakia. But now, as then, Cuban support for the Soviet action was not simply the result of Moscow's dictates. Like several military regimes in the Third World, including the Ethiopian Dergue and for a time the Somali junta, the Afghan government was seen by Castro as a progressive force, not merely because it was aligned with Moscow but because it was carrying out a programme of social reforms in an immensely poor and backward society. In an interview in 1985, he asserted, 'I believe that Afghanistan was one of those places in the world where a revolution was becoming more and more necessary'. The collapse of the regime, he argued, would destroy this on-going revolution and hand the country over to pro-Western fundamentalists. As with Czechoslovakia, the cause of instability in Afghanistan was blamed on the machinations of the CIA rather than on its internal contradictions. The Soviet invasion of Afghanistan, as of Czechoslovakia, was therefore justified on more important grounds than sovereignty. As Castro put it, 'I think Afghanistan can be a non-aligned country, but one where the revolutionary regime is maintained. If a solution is sought that is based on the idea that Afghanistan should go back to the old regime and sacrifice the revolution, then, unfortunately, I don't think there will be peace there for a long time.'[19] For all his genuine belief that the Kabul regime had to be defended at all costs, Castro must have been well aware that his support for the Soviet action undid much of his effort to become a Third World leader. It was enough to deprive him of a seat on the UN Security Council that would have gone to him in all likelihood as Chairman of the Non-Aligned Movement.

The setback coincided with renewed tensions with the United States. Castro had continued to seek a *rapprochement* with Washington that would not cripple his efforts to build alliances in the Third World. In the first two years of the Carter administration the Cuban leaders had made strenuous attempts to improve relations with the United States; the result was an agreement to set up interest sections in Havana and Washington and a series of accords over fishing rights. Castro's offer to allow Cuban exiles to visit relatives on the island and to begin the release of political prisoners, however, was not reciprocated by the Americans. Indeed, the Carter administration was sending out confusing signals; on the one hand, it showed itself willing to improve relations with Havana, and, on the other, it was insisting on concessions on Cuba's part, such as the withdrawal of its troops from Angola, that the Cuban leaders could hardly be expected to make unilaterally. The US demand for Cuban disengagement from Africa provoked Castro into one of his defiant bursts of moral righteousness. Speaking to the National Assembly of People's Power in December 1977, he reminded delegates of the double standards of the United States:

> What moral basis can the United States have to speak about Cuban troops in Africa? What moral basis can a country have whose troops are on every continent . . . ? What moral basis can the United States have to speak about our troops in Africa when their own troops are stationed right here on our own national territory, at the Guantánamo naval base? . . . It would be ridiculous for us to tell the United States government that, in order for relations between Cuba and the United States to be resumed or improved, it would have to withdraw its troops from the Philippines, or Turkey, or Greece, or Okinawa, or South Korea.[20]

Between 1979 and 1981, when Reagan assumed the presidency, tensions between Cuba and the United States rose to their highest pitch since the missile crisis of 1962. The main trouble centred on attempts by disaffected Cubans to leave the island. A spate of maritime hijackings had taken place against which the US authorities had acted faint-heartedly. In April 1980, a small group of Cubans crashed a truck through the gates of the Peruvian Embassy in Havana with the aim of asking for asylum and a Cuban policeman was killed in the crossfire. Irked by the failure of the Peruvians to hand over the gatecrashers, the authorities withdrew all their guards and a few days later almost 10,000 would-be refugees had entered the Embassy. Carter exacerbated the situation by stating that the United States would welcome these 'freedom-loving' Cubans with open arms. The Cuban leaders retaliated by authorising the mass exodus of disaffected citizens; in a sea-lift operation organised by Miami-based exiles with the agreement of the Cuban authorities, thousands of small boats sailed across to the port of Mariel to pick up the crowds of Cubans who had applied to leave the country. There were violent clashes between government supporters and the would-be refugees, known as the *gusanos* or worms. More than four months passed and over 100,000 Cubans emigrated before the sea-lift was suspended after Cuba and the United States agreed to resume negotiations.

The Mariel episode was a traumatic event for Castro; he was clearly taken by surprise at the scale of disaffection that it revealed. Moreover, it coincided with a period of deep private mourning. His constant companion and aide for the previous twenty-three years, Celia Sánchez, one of several remarkable women who had rallied to Castro's side in the mid-fifties, had died of lung cancer three months previously. Castro had lived with her on and off since they had met in the Sierra, though he kept moving from one abode to another, both for security reasons and out of a restless habit he had acquired even before the guerrilla campaign. By all accounts, Celia Sánchez had furnished some sort of domestic framework for the eccentric and irregular life Castro chose to lead, and quite possibly she had also provided an emotional stability that helped to ground his volatile nature. There was no obvious sign, however, that this personal loss had affected his political judgement, as some commentators have suggested.[21] On the contrary, Castro was able to turn a potentially damaging incident to his advantage. The extensive coverage given to the exodus of the Peruvian Embassy and Mariel people by the international media and the tales of woe told to US journalists by the newly arrived emigrants was very bad publicity for the Revolution. Yet Castro called the US bluff by mobilising such mass support for the regime that it clearly gave the lie to claims that there was widespread disaffection among the Cuban population.

He also managed to create a bigger headache for the US government by allowing several thousand people with minor criminal records to join the exodus. Castro had dismissed the self-appointed refugees as the dregs of society or the 'lumpen' elements of Cuba, but the motives of many if not the majority of the emigrants were no different from those of others who left the Caribbean islands and Central America to seek a better life in the United States.[22]

Castro's language in the public forum in this period revealed how much he had been rattled by the incident. There was no lack of motives for exasperation at the behaviour of the US government which had first failed to respond to Cuban overtures about the emigration problem and then happily turned the whole episode against the Cuban regime. In a speech in June, Castro denied that anyone convicted of a violent crime had been allowed to leave but accused the United States of sheltering the real criminals, those Batista henchmen responsible for murder and torture. Angrily he declared, 'Well, let them receive the lumpen now, the thieves of chickens and sheep and pigs and a few other things. Why the former and not the latter? Where is the morality in all this? . . . It's pure hypocrisy.'[23] The Mariel affair, however, did suggest that the Cuban leaders were out of touch with the feelings of many of their fellow citizens. The subsequent lifting of rationing on many food items and the introduction of free farmers' markets were the most visible by-product of this traumatic episode.

The advent of the Reagan administration in 1981 brought about a new low in US–Cuban relations. Cuba was seen by the new US government as a Soviet surrogate, and any re-opening of negotiations between the two countries was made dependent on the impossible demand that Cuba abandon its Soviet connection. Reagan further refused to renew the fishing agreement of 1977 and tightened the trade embargo on Cuba. In spite of the new burst of Cold War rhetoric emanating from the White House, Castro and the Cuban leaders continued quietly to seek talks with the United States without making any preconditions. Partly in order to further this process, Cuba drastically cut down on its military aid to Nicaragua and the Salvadorean rebels and began calling for a political solution in El Salvador after the 1981 offensive of the Farabundi Martí Liberation

Movement failed to dislodge the US-backed government army.

The Cuban leaders' fear of the bellicose intentions of the Reagan administration seemed to be borne out when US marines invaded Grenada in 1983. The pretext for the invasion was the breakdown in law and order after a palace coup had deposed and murdered Castro's friend and ally Maurice Bishop. Cuban military advisers and construction workers were given orders to resist the marines and, indeed, fighting took place for the first time between regular troops on both sides. The outnumbered Cubans, in particular the building workers, inflicted substantial casualties on the marines, suggesting that American troops would have no smooth passage should they attempt to invade Cuba.[24] The events in Grenada renewed fears of a US invasion under the militantly anti-Cuban administration of Reagan and prompted the creation of civilian militias to share the defence of the island with the regular armed forces. The US intervention was a new blow to Castro's hopes for an anti-imperialist alliance in the Caribbean basin. His other ally in the area, the Jamaican Michael Manley, had been defeated in the 1980 elections by the pro-Western conservative, Edward Seaga. Most of the English-speaking countries in the Caribbean, for their part, had either actively supported or passively accepted the US action.

Cuba's loss of influence in the Caribbean in the mid-eighties was counterbalanced by renewed opportunities for political and trading links with Latin America. The Falklands or Malvinas War of 1982 had revived an old anti-colonial spirit in the continent which could not fail to be in Cuba's favour. Castro had sent a message of support to the junta in Argentina offering miiitary aid. The collapse of the military dictatorships in Argentina and then in Brazil, combined with new perceptions about the need for regional co-operation among many Latin American governments, helped to end Cuba's isolation. By 1987, Cuba had restored diplomatic relations with most of the continent and trade and credits were flowing between the island and the big economic powers of the region such as Brazil, Mexico, Venezuela, and Argentina. Further afield, Cuba had established trading links with several Western

European countries, notably Spain, whose socialist government extended substantial guaranteed credit to the island.
The new openings, especially to industrialised countries with
access to high technology, were a vital component of Cuba's
foreign policy strategy in the eighties. If the United States
under Reagan and later Bush were not prepared to lift
the economic blockade, Cuba would search for sources
of capital goods elsewhere, in particular in the EEC and
Japan.[25]

Encouraged by the signs of regional co-operation on
the Latin American continent, Castro turned his considerable talent for public relations to the dire problem
of Third World debt. During the seventies, the West
had lent millions of dollars indiscriminately to the Third
World and in particular to Latin America in an attempt
to avoid an international recession by recycling the sur-
pluses generated by oil price rises. The debt that had
accumulated by the early eighties began to outstrip the
capacity of many countries even to make the interest
payments. In the first six years of the decade, the Third
World transferred to the West about \$321 billion in
repayments of principal and \$325 billion in interest re-
payments, the two together amounting to about 5 per
cent of their annual GNP.[26] The strain on their economies, exacerbated by the stringent conditions imposed on
many governments by the IMF in exchange for further
loans, was borne above all by the millions of destitute
people in the Third World. The first outward sign of
the looming crisis was the announcement by Mexico in
1982 that it could no longer maintain its interest payments.

Castro's new war-cry was not a mere piece of opportunism. The problem of Third World debt went to
the heart of his long-standing campaign to restructure
the relations between North and South. Furthermore,
he was convinced that the growing debt crisis would
create the conditions for the fulfilment of his old dream
of Latin American unity. It was also an opportunity,
now that his term of office as Chairman of the Non-
Aligned Movement had come to an end, to restore his
claim to the moral leadership of the Third World after
the Afghanistan setback. In a series of impassioned and

closely argued speeches and interviews, Castro became the most articulate advocate of the cancellation of Third World debt. He defended his case on both moral and practical grounds. The survival of Latin America, he argued, hinged on finding a solution to the debt crisis, which was 'the key problem of our time'. He maintained that the debt was so high that it was no longer payable.[27] Any attempt to impose greater sacrifices on the people of the Third World in order to continue the repayments was also politically unsafe, resulting in widespread revolt. In any case, he argued, it was morally unacceptable that underdeveloped countries should be financing the industrialised economies; he calculated that in 1984, largely because of debt repayments, Latin America made a net transfer of $26,700 million to the developed West.

The solution he proposed attempted to bridge two of the major problems facing the world, poverty and the arms race. If the creditor states were to reduce their military expenditure by as little as 12 per cent, the Third World debt could be cancelled by the simple expedient, for instance, of using the savings to issue long-term government bonds to bail out the banks responsible for the loans. A more drastic cut in arms spending, on the other hand, would not only eliminate the debt problem but also pay for a new international economic order that would be to the benefit of all. Castro repeatedly stressed the growing inequality of trade relations between the developed and less developed world. The Third World, he argued, was being impoverished by the widening gap between the price of manufactured goods it was forced to import from the developed economies and the price of its own exports to those economies. He calculated that between 1980 and 1984 alone, the Third World's purchasing power fell by almost 22 per cent. If to this were added the high rates of US interest, the consequent flight of capital from the Third World, the overvaluation of the dollar, the practice of dumping and the rise of the protectionist policies in the West, then Latin America, for one, was being despoiled of thousands of millions of dollars year after year. The cancellation of the debt and the establishment

of fair trade relations, Castro added somewhat disingenuously, would also favour the developed nations by
providing them with a huge new market in the Third
World.[28]

Castro's strategy on Third World debt, therefore, envisaged
the formation of a cartel of several debtor nations that
would use the threat of non-payment or a moratorium
on debt repayments as a bargaining tool to reduce arms
spending and to negotiate new terms of trade between
North and South. It was a long way from the strategy
of the sixties of spreading Cuba's revolutionary model
to the continent. Indeed, Castro seemed to show some
disillusionment about the possibility of revolution or socialism in one country. The strain of twenty-five years of
efforts to develop the Cuban economy in virtual isolation
and the desperate conditions imposed on the Sandinista
government may perhaps have been in his mind when he
declared to the Latin American Federation of journalists
in 1985,

> I believe that the cancellation of the debt and the
> establishment of the New International Economic
> Order is much more important than two, three or
> four isolated revolutions . . . A revolution in poverty
> is better than the system of exploitation, but you
> can't meet the enormous needs that have accumu-
> lated in all our countries . . . with social changes
> alone.[29]

Castro's eloquence on the theme of world debt bore little
relation to his ability to influence events. In the first half
of the eighties Cuba needed to raise few loans from the
West and could afford the repayments; ironically, the
Cuban authorities were renowned for the seriousness
with which they dealt with their contractual obligations.
Moreover, the Cuban economy was cushioned from the
worst effects of the Western market by its special relationship with Comecon, though this created problems of
a different kind. Nor did Castro carry much weight among
the governments of the big Latin American countries
which continued in their attempts to renegotiate their
loan debts independently of one another, encouraged
or leant on by the United States. Only Peru in 1985,

under the government of Alan García, made a stand against the terms of its debt repayments, refusing to pay back more than 10 per cent of its annual exports. In the wake of Black Monday, 19 October 1987, when the world's stock markets crashed, the rhetoric of resistance against the debt-service burden among the top Latin American countries rose a few decibels, but their governments failed once again to agree on a debtors' cartel.

It would be wrong, however, to underestimate Castro's influence in Latin America. His proposals for the solution of the debt problem may have had only the force of a moral appeal but it was difficult to avoid the conclusion that, as the debt crisis deepened, some form of united action by the Latin American countries was inevitable. Castro also had a wide audience among many sections of the Latin American population. He not only enjoyed prestige as the most determined opponent of American hegemony on the continent but he was also gaining popularity in the fast-growing movement for social justice within the Latin American Church. During his visit to Chile in 1971, and later in Jamaica and in Nicaragua, Castro had supported the call for a strategic alliance between Christians and Marxists.

The Church in Cuba had not had any roots among large sections of the population; Castro claimed that there had not been a single church in the countryside, where 70 per cent of Cubans used to live.[30] His own experience of the Christian Brothers' and Jesuit education had not endeared him to Christianity and as a self-proclaimed Marxist-Leninist he was of course an atheist. Nevertheless, relations between the Revolutionary regime and the Church had improved considerably since the clash of 1960–1. The lowest point in Church–state relations had occurred after the Bay of Pigs invasion in 1961 when the regime had banned religious education in public schools, closed down religious schools, and expelled dozens of priests in response to the covert support given by members of the clergy to the invasion attempt. The Second Vatican Council of 1962–5, with its stress on social reform, had paved the way for a new dialogue and the Cuban Church had become increasingly reconciled to the Revolution, despite its almost total loss of power and privilege.

In Latin America, however, the Church was the most influential institution among ordinary people, and from the mid-sixties many of its sections had begun to espouse demands for political reform and justice for the poor and oppressed. No revolutionary movement could therefore afford to reject or ignore it. The Sandinista revolution in Nicaragua, for example, was based on a close alliance between socialism and Christianity. Castro now claimed to find not only an identical spirit of austerity and self-sacrifice between the two movements but a common political objective. 'From a strictly political point of view . . . ,' he said in an interview with the Brazilian priest Frei Betto in 1985,

I believe that it is possible for Christians to be Marxists as well, and to work together with the Marxist Communists to transform the world. The important thing is that, in both cases, they be honest revolutionaries who want to end the exploitation of man by man and to struggle for a fair distribution of social wealth, equality, fraternity and the dignity of all human beings.[31]

It was significant that Frei Betto's interview became a best-seller in Latin America.

Indeed, Castro's call for unity between Christians and Communists and his campaign over Third World debt had a deep moral resonance in Latin America. His much-publicised words on poverty, exploitation, repression, and nationalism touched many chords beyond the small circles of the Left. Unlike most other Latin American statesmen he was free to voice the widespread aversion to the United States. In fact, he consciously sought the role of the anti-colonial conscience of Latin America and the Third World. Cuba's commitment to the cause of the Third World was evident in its relatively massive aid to nations in many parts of the world. Castro's popularity was due not only to what he said but also to the way in which he said it. His power of rhetoric and flamboyant style captured the imagination of the world's mass media and ensured that Cuba received an attention out of all proportion to its international importance.

Castro's influence abroad, however, was severely curtailed by a widespread perception that Cuba was a Soviet surrogate. Although it is true that the Cuban leaders were able to act foreign policy was not independent of Moscow. Furthermore, Cuba's own internal problems suggested that it was not a model to be followed elsewhere. Indeed, in the mid-eighties, Castro once again felt obliged to turn his attention to domestic politics and bend his efforts to resolve the growing internal contradictions of the Revolution.

. . .

NOTES AND REFERENCES

1. Granma Weekly Review (*GWR*), 7 May 1972
2. For a discussion of these issues, see Domínguez J 'Cuba in the International Arena', *Latin American Research Review*, XXIII(1) 1988
3. Castro F 1983 *Conversaciones con periodistas norteamericanos y franceses*. Política, Havana
4. E.g., Elliott J M and Dymally M M 1986 *Fidel Castro: Nothing Can Stop the Course of History*. Pathfinder, New York, pp. 108–20; Betto F 1987 *Fidel and Religion*. Weidenfeld & Nicolson, London, p. 299
5. For Noriega, see Castro's interview with NBC's Maria Shriver in *GWR*, 13 March 1988, and for the Malvinas, *Granma*, 3 May 1982
6. Castro Ruz F 1972 *Fidel in Chile*. International Publishers, New York, p. 119
7. Castro Ruz 1972 p. 213
8. Taber M (ed.) 1983 *Fidel Castro Speeches*. Pathfinder, New York, vol. 2, pp. 13–14
9. Castro Ruz 1972 pp. 136 and 220
10. Reed S L 'Participation in Multinational Organizations and Programs in the Hemisphere', in Blasier C and Mesa-Lago C (eds) 1979 *Cuba in the World*. University of Pittsburgh, pp. 297–312
11. For further discussion of US policy towards Cuba, see Morley M H 1987 *Imperial State and Revolution: the United States and Cuba, 1952–1986*. Cambridge University Press, Cambridge
12. García Márquez G 'Cuba in Angola: Operation Carlotta', in Taber M (ed.) 1981 *Fidel Castro's Speeches: Cuba's International Foreign Policy 1975–80*. Pathfinder, New York, p. 353

13. *GRW*, 9 July 1972
14. E.g., Castro F 1977 *Fidel Castro habla con Barbara Walters*. Carlos Valencia Editores, Colombia, p. 53; and Shevchenko A *Breaking with Moscow* New York, Alfred A Knopf 1985 p. 272
15. Smith W S 1987, New York, W W Norton and Co. p. 130
16. Castro's speech on 26 July 1979, in Taber 1981 pp. 293–309
17. Taber 1981 p. 167
18. Erisman M H 1985 *Cuba's International Relations: the Anatomy of a Nationalistic Foreign Policy*. Westview, Boulder, Co, pp. 128–9
19. Elliott and Dymally 1986 pp. 18 and 183
20. Fidel Castro, speech in Taber 1981 p. 253
21. E.g., Bourne P 1987 London, Macmillan p. 295
22. Bach R L 'Socialist Construction and Cuban Emigration: Explorations into Mariel', *Cuban Studies* 15(2) Summer 1985
23. *Granma*, 16 June 1980
24. Erisman 1985 pp. 146 and 156, n 41
25. Stubbs J 1989 *Cuba: the Test of Time*. Latin America Bureau, London, pp. 131–6
26. Roddick J 1988 *The Dance of the Millions: Latin America and the Debt Crisis*. Latin America Bureau, London, p. 3
27. Betto 1987 pp. 301 and 297
28. Castro F 1985 *La Cancelación de la deuda externa y el nuevo orden económico internacional como única alternativa verdadera. Otros asuntos de interés político e histórico*. Editora Política, Havana, pp. 101, 122–5, 156–7; Betto 1987 pp. 299–300
29. Speech to Fourth Congress of FELAP, 6 July 1985, quoted in O'Brien P 'The Debt Cannot be Paid: Castro and the Latin American Debt', *Bulletin of Latin American Research*, 5(1) 1986, p. 56
30. Betto 1987 p. 181
31. Op. cit., p. 276

Chapter 8

STRAIGHTENING THE RUDDER

In February 1986, Castro rose before the delegates of the Third Congress of the Cuban Communist Party to launch a new offensive on the domestic front, ponderously entitled the 'Rectification of errors and negative trends'. It marked his return to the centre of the political stage in Cuba after a decade or so during which his presence had loomed less large on the domestic scene. His speech vilified talk of liberalising the economy and attacked corruption, corporatism, materialism, and selfishness in Cuban society; it pressed for higher productivity and lower consumption and appealed for a return to egalitarian moral values. In short, Castro was calling for more sacrifices on the part of the Cuban people.

The immediate background to the new campaign was the worsening economic situation in Cuba in the mid-eighties. After the disappointing growth rates of the sixties, the economy had recovered in the following decade. In the first half of the seventies, the global social product (GSP) had risen by an average of 14.8 per cent, to slow down to an annual rate of 4.6 per cent between 1976 and 1979. By the mid-eighties, however, a sharp decline was evident, exacerbated by unfavourable weather conditions, low productivity, inadequate planning, and the tightening of the US economic blockade by the Reagan administration. By 1986, Cuba had a record deficit of over $199 million and a foreign debt of $3.87 billion, 6.9 per cent higher than in 1985, while GSP grew by only 1.4 per cent over the previous year. Furthermore, credit from the West fell because of Cuba's unusual inability to service its accumulated debt of over $6 billion.[1]

The ups and downs of Cuba's economic performance had not affected the state's considerable investment in social reform, foreign aid, and military involvement abroad. Indeed,

146

underpinned by long-term credit and trade agreements with the Soviet Union, the Cubans had achieved standards of health and literacy rivalling those of developed countries. The infant mortality rate, a common yardstick of development, had dropped from 60 per thousand live births in 1958 to 13.3 in the mid-eighties. Whereas on the eve of the Revolution there was only one doctor for every 5,000 Cubans, the ratio had fallen some thirty years later to one per 400. Average life expectancy had risen to 74 from 57 and only 2 per cent of the population was illiterate compared to 24 per cent in 1958. All children of primary-school age now attended school whereas only 56 per cent had done so before the Revolution.[2] The bare figures conceal the extent of social and economic change in Cuba. The countryside in particular enjoyed the benefits of the massive injection of state funds. Not only had the traditional pattern of class relations been swept aside by expropriation and nationalisation, but the old blight of unemployment and underemployment had also been virtually eliminated. Small rural towns of between 500 and 2,000 inhabitants, endowed with running water, electricity, clinics and schools, now dotted the countryside where once much of the peasant population had been scattered about in jerry-built huts surrounded by tiny plots of land. Latifundia had given way to state farms, state-assisted co-operatives, and small but productive private holdings, though the reorganisation of the agrarian sector had not taken place without trauma. There was no poverty or disease of the kind that ravaged much of Latin America, including the most developed of its economies. The Cubans had access to an unrivalled breadth of social and recreational services and educational opportunities. At the same time, Cuban medical personnel, engineers, teachers, and military advisers were working in dozens of poor countries as part of the government's generous foreign aid programme. And Cuban troops were about to fight a decisive battle in Angola against the South African army.

The most conspicuous shortfall in Cuban society was the lack of consumer goods. Castro was adamant that the success of the Revolution had to be judged in part at least on the basis of health, housing, and education and not in terms of the availability of consumer goods. The very phrase 'living standards' drew Castro's scorn as he railed against the 'terrible national egoism' that he felt it implied. To the customary applause, he declared, 'To tell the truth, we would like ten or twenty metres more of cloth per capita, but that is not our problem at the moment; our problem is development, our problem is the future. We can't mortgage the future for ten metres of cloth!'[3]

None the less, since the lean years of the late sixties, the supply and range of basic consumer goods had improved considerably. This was the result mainly of economic growth but it was helped also by the new policy of allowing goods to be sold at a higher price in state-run 'parallel markets' and by the institution in 1980 of the 'free farmers' markets' where the private small holders could sell off their surplus at unpegged prices. These liberalising measures were part of an attempt in the mid-seventies to introduce a limited number of market mechanisms into the economy. After the disastrous sugar campaign of 1970, Cuba's war-type economy of the late sixties had been modified; a new framework called the System of Direction and Planning of the Economy (SDPE) had been brought in, allowing a certain decentralisation of planning and management and a new range of material incentives. The aim had been to improve efficiency and stimulate production.[4]

Although Castro was careful not to criticise the new system directly, he was clearly uncomfortable with it. It was no coincidence that measures of economic liberalisation in the past had been introduced during the two occasions when Castro's model of a centralised and 'moral' economy had been under particular pressure: in 1964 after the failure of the industrialisation drive, and after the 1970 crisis. His latent mistrust of market mechanisms was strengthened in the mid-eighties when it appeared that the economy was beginning to suffer severe strains. Matters came to a head over the 1985 plan drawn up by the Central Planning Board (Juceplan) under its head, Humberto Pérez, a Moscow-trained economist. On Castro's personal intervention, the plan was overriden on the grounds that it provided for an excessively swollen budget without taking into account the economic situation in Cuba. One of the most important problems, Castro implied, had been that the decentralisation of economic decision-making had given rise to corporatist tendencies in the bureaucracy. Justifying his action, he told the National Assembly, 'during all these years, since we began our first efforts of planning and development, a sectorial spirit has reigned in all the organizations, in all the Ministries. . . a battle by each institution for the limited resources available. This criterion, this style,. . . has been declared abolished and it has been established that the plan should be everyone's plan and that the economy was the economy of everyone'.[5] Bypassing the Juceplan, Castro set up a new committee to draw up a revised plan for 1985 that drastically pared down state expenditure, gave priority to exports over imports and instituted measures to save resources. Shortly afterwards, Humberto Pérez, the technocrat most associated with the SDPE, was removed from his post and in 1986 dropped from the Politburo.

With the Rectification campaign, Castro broadened the target of his criticism. In a series of congresses between 1986 and 1987, he launched into an attack on the 'errors and negative trends' that had arisen during the previous years. At the same time he called on the Cubans to raise productivity, lower consumption, and renew voluntary labour, in particular the voluntary construction teams, the Microbrigadas. His handling of these lengthy meetings was quintessentially Castroist. He engaged delegates in a running dialogue, enquiring about the smallest details of their work and using the information provided to illustrate his broader themes. Few institutions escaped the lash of his tongue. He denounced the low productivity of Cuban industry, blaming management for allowing resources to be wasted, the technocrats for failing to carry out proper job evaluation, and workers for taking advantage of low work norms to earn excessive bonuses. He denounced the rise of a new crust of small entrepreneurs who had seized the opportunities offered by the introduction of market mechanisms such as the free farmers' markets to enrich themselves. He noted that as a result of these trends income differentials were growing and consumerism was creeping in, while voluntary labour had become devalued. In general, over the past few years, he went on, discipline had declined as well as respect for the law.[6]

As in 1970, the new campaign responded in part to mass pressure from below. By the mid-eighties a generalised feeling of disaffection had spread in particular among the urban population and was beginning to be reflected somewhat cautiously in sections of the press. Havana, as the political, administrative, and industrial centre of the island and the most populated city in Cuba, appeared to be the hotbed of these criticisms. The source of discontent was not merely the continuing problem of the poor supply of subsidised goods, the high price of produce sold on the parallel market, or the quality of services such as public transport. It was also that the sacrifices being demanded by the leaders were unequally spread. It was well known that there were people who were taking advantage of the shortages to make a handsome profit out of the new more liberal system. There were others in the administration, the military, or the state enterprises who were felt to be abusing their privileges; stories abounded about old-boy networks, rake-offs, high expense-accounts, and the use of state cars for private purposes. In a speech to the Third Party Congress, Castro took up some of these complaints, acting characteristically as a sort of self-appointed spokesman of popular discontent against the administration. His reputation as 'the synthesis of the best virtues of the people' was thereby strengthened. As a leading member of the Central Committee and a Castro protégé said at the same Congress, 'In no small number of meetings and assemblies during these past months, I have heard people regret the fact that once again it has been comrade Fidel who has had to confront the deviations and mistaken policies'.[7]

Castro's sharpest invective was directed at his old *bête noire*, the bureaucrats and technocrats. Seizing on the example of the Ministry of Construction (MINCONS), whose representatives in the hall must have squirmed in their seats at his remarks, he declared with heavy sarcasm:

> To appeal to the MINCONS and say to them. . . please build a day-care centre in Guanabacoa because there's a new factory . . . that needs a workforce and doesn't have it or has a crisis on its hands because 200 women have to pay 60, 70, or 80 pesos plus food to have their children looked after, MINCONS couldn't build a single day-care centre, not one! Because simply to ask them to build a day-care centre was enough to make them faint. . . How can you ask such a terrible thing, to build a day-care centre in Gaunabacoa with all the commitments we already have and all the projects that we never finish.

Castro's example of the day-care centre was not picked out

of the air; he meant to drive home the connection between social needs and economic development that was the essence of his 'moral economy'.

Indeed, moral images dominated his speeches about the economy. Conjuring up a rather tasteless image in the heat of his speech, he accused some of Cuba's technocrats and bureaucrats of, 'suffering from and transmitting a sort of ideological AIDS . . . that was destroying the Revolution's defences'.[8] This new bureaucratic disease, according to Castro, was no less than the spread of a 'capitalist or petty-bourgeois' spirit among people who appeared very well-versed in Marxism but who mistakenly pinned their faith on market mechanisms, forgetting the primacy of revolutionary consciousness.[9] In the past, Castro had repeatedly attacked bureaucratic deviations. His renewed offensive in the Rectification campaign hinted at the rise since the seventies of a new layer of managers in the administration and the state enterprises closely associated with the reformist measures of the SDPE. These favoured greater autonomy for management, plant-level profit schemes, material incentives, wage differentials, and a greater number of consumer outlets for skilled workers.

Castro's offensive, however, was not against the SDPE itself; he merely argued that it had been applied inefficiently (and in some cases corruptly) and that it had gone too far. The Rectification campaign therefore was neither a return to the 'war economy' of the 1966–70 period nor a rejection of the new system of economic management but an attempt to restore a balance between the two. It was significant that despite his attack on private entrepreneurship within Cuba (the peasants' markets were closed in 1986) Castro did not question the official policy of encouraging joint-venture agreements between Cuban state enterprises and private foreign companies. Behind Rectification lay the compelling need to respond to the economic crisis in Cuba in the mid-eighties without sacrificing the principles of the Revolution. Castro evidently believed that the price of any further economic liberalisation was too high for Cuba: on one hand, it was demobilising the people and on the other it was undermining the egalitarian basis of the Revolution. In the conditions of persistent underdevelopment and the continuing blockade by the United States, Castro believed the government could not afford to relinquish its control over the economy, nor could the Cuban people relax or 'indulge' in consumerism. The survival of the Revolution depended on generating the highest possible level of surplus for investment in defence, overseas commitments, and social welfare. In a declining economy this meant tightening the national belt even further and boosting productivity without raising wages. In his opinion, only a partial return to more centralised controls and a restoration of moral incentives alongside material rewards could ensure the right equilibrium.

Castro's stern words throughout the second half of the eighties were not those of a revolutionary puritan or an ageing Stalinist clinging to outworn dogma, as some commentators have suggested.[10] They were based on a perception that the system of economic management introduced in the mid-seventies was not working well and that, while it had to be reformed, the Cuban leaders had also to renew their traditional instruments of decision-making and mobilisation. Castro had always believed that the economy had to be directed centrally; as he put it in 1988, 'There is a key principle of socialism which is especially valid for a developing country: the centralisation of decisions on the use of resources in the economic field.'[11] But he had had to give way when his own model had come under strain. In fact, there was nothing new about Rectification. It was the same method of straightening the rudder to 'correct' the course of the Revolution that Castro had employed ever since he had come to power: after the failure of the industrialisation campaign in the early sixties, during the radical phase between 1966 and 1970, and following the crisis of 1970. All four policy shifts were a response to internal and external pressures, of which the most important was the pressure of the world market.

Similar strains, though of an altogether different magnitude, affected the Soviet bloc in the mid-eighties, prompting a section of the Soviet leadership headed by Gorbachev to launch a programme of economic reforms or *perestroika* (restructuring). The Rectification campaign in Cuba could be said to have begun before *perestroika* in that Castro launched his first broadside against inefficiency in 1984. Both Castro and Gorbachev were pursuing the same objective, to increase productivity and economic efficiency in a declining economy, but the means they used differed because the obstacles they faced were different in each country. *Perestroika* sought to weaken the centralised control of the state over the economy and introduce a radical set of market mechanisms to stimulate rationalisation and productivity. Rectification, on the other hand, strengthened state control and centralised planning over the economy. The accompanying policy of *glasnost* or openness in the Soviet Union was above all a campaign to break up the entrenched interests in the Party and the bureaucracy that were blocking reform. In a small and centralised society like Cuba, no section of the Party or the bureaucracy had formed an autonomous power base such as those found in the Soviet Union. It is true that Castro used a similar method to bring to heel what he saw as vested bureaucratic interests. Like Gorbachev, he encouraged criticism from below in order to shake up the intermediate layers of the Cuban leadership. Like the Soviet leader, he orchestrated these voices of censure, conducting affairs from the speaker's rostrum, as a sort of chairman and devil's advocate rolled into one. Often, as in the congress of the Young Communists (UJC) in the spring of 1987, Castro insisted that his ministers attend meetings in which they were subjected to forceful criticism from rank-and-file delegates. Indeed, this had always been Castro's way of dealing with internal conflicts within the Party and society at large. In an interview with the NBC in 1988, he claimed, 'we have *glasnost* here, we have always had it. No party in the world has been more self-critical than the Communist Party of Cuba. None. Examine our history and you will see *glasnost* on a large scale.'[12]

Yet there was an essential difference between the two processes. Whereas Soviet *glasnost* had opened up a Pandora's box of demands that threatened to undermine the fragile stability of the USSR, the Cuban version, if it could be called by the same name, was a decidedly controlled and limited affair. It appeared that dissent was tolerated to the extent that it suited the leadership. At a time when Castro was anxious to root out inefficiency and petty corruption among officials at all levels, criticism was allowed to flourish as long as it was directed against malpractice or bureaucratic immobility. But criticism that questioned the principles of the Revolution itself was hardly permissible. Cubans who had been jailed under a law that made oppositional activities treasonable were now being released, but there was still a long way to go before open dissent against official policy could freely emerge outside the institutions of the state. The oblique complaints in the bolder columns of the press could hardly compare with the critical dialogue that was taking place in the Soviet Union.

Indeed, it could be said that the only truly investigative reporter in Cuba was Castro. He still went round the island, though less often than in the sixties, his keen eye picking out evidence of abuses and inefficiencies. Where he approved criticism, it poured forth. During his walk-abouts, people mobbed him for solutions to small local problems, knowing that his word was the administration's command. Castro had surrounded himself with a small group of about twenty bright young technicians and administrators who acted as his personal assistants and troubleshooters. This Co-ordinating and Support Group had become the training-ground for future government leaders, and several cabinet ministers had been drawn from its ranks. It suggested once again that though he did not ignore official channels, Castro's instincts had always been towards central control and direct action. 'In my office,' he said in an interview with the *Washington Post* in 1985, 'I have 20 comrades who are on the road constantly visiting factories, hospitals, schools, co-ordinating, helping everyone and they are not inspectors, they are people who go round, see how the situation is, co-ordinate one organism with another.'[13] Moreover, he was the only consistent source of statistics about the economy and the society. It was mainly Castro who, from the rostrum and the television screen, informed the people what was going on in Cuba.

Nevertheless, it would be wrong to assume from this that once again, as in the sixties, he exercised almost unlimited power. An intense debate took place within the party and the leadership before and during the Rectification campaign and spread downwards through the institutions and the local assemblies to the street. The new programme was almost certainly the result of a consensus arising in part from divergencies among the leadership and pressures from below. The discussions were often heated, leading to open disagreements between top officials and once between Castro and one of his ministers in the National Assembly itself.[14] If heterodox political views were still considered beyond the pale in the late eighties, there was a much more critical debate over policy-making within the boundaries of the Revolution than there had been in the two previous decades.

Nor did Castro's return to prominence on the domestic stage signal a power shift within the regime. Instead, it was a renewal of the populist style of the sixties in the service of a new social mobilisation. The system of economic administration set in place in the seventies, stressing decentralised management and material incentives, did not require the same sort of charismatic leadership that accompanied campaigns for greater patriotic exertion. As the supreme commander and the most effective communicator among the leadership, it inevitably fell to Castro to lead the offensive that he had almost certainly initiated in the first place. While there was a dramatic turnover of middle-ranking party members and managers and officials in the economic ministries in the wake of the Rectification campaign, the changes of personnel among the top leadership did not suggest that there had been any serious divisions; rather, they indicated a shift in emphasis similar to the practice of cabinet reshuffles; the ministers who were sacked were those most closely associated with the policy failures. In the 1986 elections to the Politburo, of the twenty-seven members of the 1980–5 Politburo nine lost their seats but retained their position in the Central Committee, one died, one was transferred to the Secretariat and one retired because of old age.

The picture of Castro made popular by some of the Western press as an eccentric holding-out against the inevitable forces of modernisation epitomised by Gorbachev was thus a distorted one. The campaigns for *perestroika* and Rectification arose from different political needs and traditions, as Castro pointed out in his speech to the National Assembly on the occasion of Gorbachev's visit.[15] In contrast to the Soviet Union, Cuba was a small and relatively homogeneous society whose members could still be mobilised to perform extraordinary feats of collective endeavour when called on by the regime. Whereas the Soviet reformers saw liberalisation as a means of releasing energies blocked by the dead weight of bureaucracy, the Cuban leadership believed on the contrary that they needed to strengthen their grip on the economy and on society in order to motivate their citizens to work harder and to defend the Revolution against the threat of American aggression. Rectification was their response to the three-way vice of economic decline, popular dissatisfaction, and the enduring need for the state to cream off a substantial portion of the national surplus.

For all their dissimilarities, *perestroika* and Rectification were closely bound together. Castro may have dismissed the idea of a Cuban *perestroika* on the grounds that it was inappropriate, but he could not escape the effects of Gorbachev's reforms. *Glasnost* and *perestroika* were trendy; the call for a greater effort that was at the heart of the Rectification campaign was not. One of the new slogans associated with the campaign, *Ahora sí podemos construir el socialismo* (translated in the official Cuban daily *Granma* as 'Now we are really going to build socialism') sounded a rather jaded note, as if all the sacrifices in the past had been in vain, and it became the target of much popular criticism. Among a few sections of the Party such as some of the old pre-Revolutionary Communists and some of the Young Communists there was consider-able, albeit muted, admiration for Gorbachev; indeed, a Soviet leader for once appeared to have upstaged Castro.

More importantly, the restructuring of Soviet economic management had serious implications for the special rela-tionship between the two countries. Gorbachev intended to introduce more cost-effective principles in the Soviet Union's international trading links. During his visit to Cuba in April 1989, he gave an unequivocal warning of the new approach: 'As life moves ahead, new demands are being made on the quality of our interaction. This applies particularly to economic contacts – they should be more dynamic and effective and bring greater returns for both our countries, both our peoples.'[16] Henceforth, Cuban economic agencies would have to deal less with the Soviet bureaucracy than directly with buyers and suppliers acting on new criteria of profitability. The Soviet Union would seek to restore a greater balance of trade between the two countries and the concealed price subsidies built into Cuban–Soviet trade would be reduced. This hidden agenda lay beneath the much fanfared twenty-five-year treaty of co-operation signed jointly by Gorbachev and Castro during the former's visit to Cuba and the protocol agreed between the two countries shortly afterwards.

However, the most serious effect for Cuba of Gorbachev's 'new political thinking' was his tacit withdrawal from Third

World politics. In the late sixties, Castro had criticised the Soviet Union for its lukewarm support for national liberation struggles such as that waged in Vietnam. Nevertheless, under Brezhnev in the seventies, the Kremlin had been heavily involved in military and commercial aid to Soviet-aligned countries, viewing the Third World as an arena of East–West confrontation. Gorbachev explicitly rejected this conception of international relations. He argued that the problems of poverty and conflict in the underdeveloped world could only be solved by concerted action between the superpowers and they had to be subordinated therefore to the primary objective of *détente* between East and West. Though he claimed there was an important role for Latin America in the process of *détente*, it was clear that the Third World was to be a more or less passive spectator of superpower negotiations. Moreover, Gorbachev hinted that he was more interested in the trading potential of Latin American countries that in their political colour.[17]

The growing convergence between Moscow and Washington in the late eighties was welcomed by Castro to the extent that it led to international *détente*. A substantial cut in arms expenditure would release money that could be made available for development aid or to underwrite Third World debt. US–Soviet *détente* would also pave the way for a renewal of US–Cuban relations and the dismantling of the economic siege of the island. However, he did not believe that the United States had changed its spots. A strategic retreat of the Soviet Union from the Third World would leave Cuba and other countries such as Nicaragua dangerously exposed to American harassment, in his opinion. In a speech in 1988, on the thirty-second anniversary of the Granma landing, he had declared, referring to the United States as the empire, 'We sincerely support the peace policy of the Soviet Union. But peace has different meanings for different countries. It's almost certain that the way the empire conceives peace is among the powerful, peace with the Soviet Union and war with the small, socialist, revolutionary, progressive or simply independent countries of the Third World.'[18] He made his disquiet evident during Gorbachev's visit to Cuba in April 1989. Contrasting the revolutionary process in Cuba and Russia, he indulged in a sardonic, somewhat incautious dig at the Soviet Union's expense, declaring that there had been no Stalinism in Cuba, 'unless I am considered... a sort of

Stalin, and in that case I would say that all my victims in our country are in excellent health'. He went on to make an implicit criticism of Gorbachev's policies: 'We know what the expression of new international political thinking means, a new mentality in handling problems. But we don't have any assurances, we still don't have them. We don't have any indication that the imperialists have adopted this new international thinking. On the contrary, we have many reasons to distrust their conduct.'[19]

The problem for Castro was not just that Moscow was pulling out of its military commitments to the Third World but that it was redefining its trading links and foreign aid programme to bring it more in line with capitalist practices. Despite his reassuring words to the contrary, Gorbachev's reforms contained a hidden menace that eventually both the security and the economic viability of Cuba might be undermined by Soviet withdrawal. Castro's ability to play off Moscow and Washington against each other would be considerably reduced now that the Soviet Union no longer saw Cuba as a lever against the United States. Gorbachev's new international policy, by downgrading the Third World as an agency for change, also threatened to erode Castro's ability to play an active role in world affairs. Cuban military missions abroad, though they were not always established at Moscow's bidding, had fitted in with Soviet strategy and had relied on its military and diplomatic support. The most spectacular of these was the Cuban operation in Angola. For thirteen years Cuban troops, backed by Soviet arms, had held together the fragile independence of Angola against the incursions of South Africa and the harassing operations of its client guerrilla organisation, Unita. The military victory of Cuban and Angolan troops over the South African army at Cuito Cuanavale in May 1988 had helped to force Pretoria into negotiations to end the conflict in Southern Africa and to recognise the independence of Namibia. Although the resulting Brazzaville Accords stemmed in large measure from the convergence of policy towards that area between Reagan and Gorbachev, the Cuban involvement had been decisive in convincing Pretoria that the cost of further military action was too high. Cuba's standing among many Third World countries, in particular among the Front Line states, was as high as it had ever been. Such prestigious operations, however, were far less likely now that the Soviet Union was drawing back from any overt political involvement in the Third World.

Indeed, at the end of the eighties, Castro's options were narrowing both at home and abroad. He was faced by increasing economic strains and growing dissatisfaction among many sections of the population exacerbated by the return of thousands of Angolan veterans. The crackdown on speculators profiting from the shortage of goods was not simply a moral gesture but was intended to reassure a restless population that the government would be fair in its treatment of all citizens. Hence the infuriated reaction of the leadership to the discovery in June 1989 that top officials of the Interior Ministry had been smuggling millions of dollars worth of Colombian cocaine into the United States. In a joint trial, one of Cuba's leading generals and hero of the Angolan campaign, Arnaldo Ochoa Sánchez, was also accused of profiteering and drug trafficking but the charges against him were less clear. Indeed, while guilty of some offences, Ochoa may have fallen foul of the leadership for being too independent in his military operations and even for voicing criticism of the Castro brothers. That the whole affair was more than just a case of individual venality on the part of a handful of officials is suggested by the wide-ranging purge of the Interior Ministry that followed the trial and execution of the four leading defendants. The fact that it was Fidel Castro who had had to order the investigation in the first place, perhaps because the accused were too high up in the echelons of the government, emphasised once again how much the health of the regime continued to depend on his authority.[20]

The trial, broadcast at length on Cuban television in an edited version, appeared to lend weight to the growing complaints among many sections of the Cuban population about the abuse of power by some officials. Popular criticism was directed not only at the paucity and poor quality of consumer goods and the inadequacy of certain public services but also at corruption among officials, epitomised by the growth of an 'old boys' network' nicknamed *sociolismo* from the Spanish word for 'partner' *socio*. The Cuban leadership was also criticised from within the party structure for its reluctance to share power. The strongest challenge on this account came from the new generation of Communists.

'We are living in a period of healthy insurgency,' its daily paper declared in August 1988. 'The scant regard paid to it gives rise often to palpable nonconformism. . . . The just desire for a more comfortable existence raises the need for the greater participation of everyone in the search for solutions to the problems of the country.'[21] The impatience of the young militants for more democracy, expressed notably in the 1987 Congress of the Young Communists, was creating tension between the two generations.[22] Indeed, the new generation betrayed little reverence towards the sacred cows of the Revolution. Castro alone continued to command enormous admiration but there were also many ordinary people who were saying that it was time he should retire. As usual he displayed his ability to disarm potential criticism by assuming the mantle of devil's advocate. In a meeting with an official youth cultural organisation, for example, Castro was reputedly shaken by the discontent expressed by young writers and artists with the policies and behaviour of the government's cultural officials. One of the youthful critics was interrupted by the powerful head of the Department of Revolutionary Orientation and Propaganda, Carlos Aldana, who complained about the rancorous atmosphere in the hall but Castro, in his turn, interrupted him and told him to listen to the criticism.[23] At the same time, Cuba appeared to have a declining importance in the eyes of the Soviet Union while remaining a target of American hostility under the new administration of George Bush. The campaign of Rectification could at best eradicate some of the corruption and inefficiency that had beset the administration of the economy and society. It might encourage further patriotic efforts on the part of many Cubans. But it could not pull off a miracle of development. It would be no exaggeration to say that the dilemmas confronting Castro and the Cuban leadership at the end of the decade, though different in kind, were as great as any they had had to face during the previous thirty years.

. . .

NOTES AND REFERENCES

1.   Azicri M 1988 *Cuba: Politics, Economics and Society*. Pinter, London, pp. 140–1 and 144–9

2. Stubbs, J 1989 p.v
3. *Granma*, 1 Dec. 1986; *Bohemia*, 14 Dec. 1984
4. Pérez H 1979 *Sobre las dificultades objetivas de la revolución. Lo que el pueblo debe saber.* Política, Havana
5. *Granma*, 5 Jan. 1985
6. Op. cit., 1 Dec. 1986
7. Carlos Aldana quoted in *Granma*, 1 Dec. 1986; the quote on Castro's reputation was extracted from *Juventud Rebelde*, 18 Sept. 1988
8. Granma Weekly Review (*GWR*), 13 Dec. 1987
9. *Granma*, 9 June 1986
10. E.g., Szulc T 1987 *Fidel: a Critical Portrait*. Hutchinson, London
11. *GWR* July 24 1988
12. Op. cit., 13 March 1988
13. *Granma*, 12 Feb. 1985
14. Author's interview with José Ramón Vidal, editor of *Juventud Rebelde*
15. *GWR*, 16 April 1989
16. Speech to the National Assembly in 1989, 'Visit of Mikhail Gorbachev to Cuba' Novosti Press, Moscow, p. 10
17. Op. cit., pp. 17 and 22
18. *GWR*, 18 Dec. 1988
19. Op. cit., 16 April 1989
20. *GWR*, 22 June and 10 July 1989; *Juventud Rebelde*, 26 June 1989; for a speculative analysis of the trials see Julia Preston, 'The Trial that Shook Cuba', *New York Review of Books* 7 December 1989
21. Cruz S 'Sí, hay arreglo', *Juventud Rebelde*, 30 Aug. to 5 Sept. 1988, p. 2
22. Author's interview with José Ramón Vidal
23. Interview with Ramón Fernández-Larrea, Sept. 1988

Chapter 9

SOCIALISM OR DEATH!

The collapse of the Communist regimes in Eastern Europe from 1989 onwards and of the Soviet Union itself at the end of 1991 was a mortal blow for the Castro regime. The Cuban economy had remained afloat largely through their support. Almost all of Cuba's trade had been with the Comecon countries, which had provided credits to cover Cuba's increasing trade deficit as well as developmental loans and massive price subsidies. By 1991, the Soviet bloc's support of Cuba was said to be equivalent to some 37 per cent of the total debt of developing nations towards donor countries.[1] The last Cuban-Soviet Trade Pact had been signed in 1991 and had envisaged a transition over a period of one year towards a new system of trade, conducted in hard currency and at world market prices. As long as the regime retained friends in high places within the Soviet state, however, some continued support could be expected. In the aftermath of the failed coup of December 1991 and the dissolution of the Soviet Union, all the regime's backers in Russia were swept from their positions of power.

The news of the coup was relayed to Castro at the end of the Panamerican Games, as the Cuban leaders were celebrating the triumph of Cuban athletes over those of the United States. Their euphoria at the news quickly gave way to concern as the coup turned into a rout, and to alarm as the Soviet Communist Party and the Soviet Union itself disintegrated.[2] Boris Yeltsin was known to be hostile towards the Cuban regime. A military leader close to the Russian leader had stated, 'Perhaps the best favour we could do to the Cuban people would be to cut off all collaboration with the Castro regime so that the island may return to the path of world civilization'.[3]

The new governments in Russia and the Commonwealth of Independent States rapidly dismantled their links with Cuba. By 1992, most Soviet personnel had left the island and in June 1993, the last of the Soviet troops, 500 Russian soldiers and families of the Motorized Infantry Brigade, which had been in Cuba since 1962, set sail for Russia. The sudden decline in Comecon trade and aid had a dramatic effect on the Cuban economy. Between 1989 and 1992, total export earnings fell by around 60 per cent and total imports by 70 per cent. By 1993 domestic economic activity had fallen some 35 per cent to 40 per cent below that of 1989.[4] During an international conference on the Missile Crisis in 1992, Castro declared that the disintegration of the Soviet Union was 'worse for us than the October Crisis', and in a speech to the National Assembly a year later he described the resulting loss of preferential trade and aid as a 'treacherous, devastating blow'.[5]

Faced with a rapidly deteriorating economy, the Cuban leadership responded with a series of piecemeal initiatives designed to fill the gap left by the collapse of Soviet and East European trade and to re-orient the economy towards new trading partners. At the beginning of 1990, Castro declared a new policy called the Special Period in Time of Peace, an adaption of wartime emergency plans drawn up when it was feared that President Reagan might institute a total naval blockade of Cuba. The measures it entailed, the reduction of food subsidies and cuts in public expenditure, were similar to those measures of adjustment common to other Third World countries at the time, except that the basic welfare of Cubans was protected to a greater extent than the poor elsewhere, as Castro was keen to point out.[6] Production was partially militarized, fuel and electricity were cut, farmers were encouraged to use oxen ('the noble ox', as Castro now described it, trying to make a virtue out of necessity) and a whole range of projects and social programmes was suspended.[7]

A Food Programme was also launched in an attempt to overcome the problems in the production and supply of foodstuffs created by the phased withdrawal of Soviet trade. It involved a huge investment of money and labour, requiring yet again the mass mobilization of volunteers, such as students, from outside the agrarian sector. Like many such initiatives in the past, it was blighted by shortages and the inadequacies of central management (the students, for example, abandoned the fields to sit for their summer exams and many of the crops rotted where they stood).[8] Should the Special Period fail or should the embargo tighten, Castro warned, Cubans would face Zero Option, total isolation from the rest of the world.

Despite the expectations it had aroused, however, the twice–postponed Fourth Congress of the Cuban Communist Party of October 1991 failed to make any far-reaching economic reforms. The 'free farmers markets' of the early eighties were not re-established and only a very limited range of private businesses of an individual and artisanal nature were sanctioned. But as the crisis deepened, the regime was forced to announce further reform measures. Production was reorganised on state–owned sugar plantations, creating smaller workforces and awarding material incentives and small plots of land for the labourers. In July 1993, the internal use of the dollar was finally legalized, after years of frenzied exchange on the black market. Yet it was a measure designed more to control the booming submerged economy, and to bring in much needed hard currency from Cubans in exile, than to stimulate production.[9] Individual businesses in a hundred further occupations already flourishing underground were sanctioned and state farms were turned into collectives. And at the beginning of 1994, Castro announced a monetary reform package eliminating state subsidies on a whole range of goods and services as well as the introduction of progressive taxation and the adoption of a convertible currency.

After the collapse of the special relationship with the Soviet Union, the economic strategy of the Cuban leadership set out to achieve a reinsertion of Cuban trade into the capitalist market. This was to be accomplished, without any fundamental reform of the domestic command economy, by finding new outlets for Cuba's traditional exports such as sugar, nickel, citrus fruit and tobacco, by expanding tourism, and by marketing the much prized biotechnological products developed in Cuba's laboratories. All these activities were beset by problems: the continued US embargo made it difficult to find new trading partners, neighbouring economies produced a similar range of traditional exports, the production of sugar and nickel depended on the import of fuel, spare parts and technology which Cuba could ill afford, and Cuba's infant pharmaceutical industry could hardly compete on the international market with multinational firms enjoying far greater resources for research and development. Indeed, the export sector needed to attract foreign capital and know-how in order to compete in the world market. To this end, the regime encouraged the growth of joint ventures with foreign capital. By the mid-nineties over a hundred major joint ventures of various forms were in operation, mostly in the tourist sector, with Cuba providing the personnel and the infrastructure and foreign firms the technology and the market.[10] Castro, always at the centre of economic decision-making, participated in the negotiations, which often had to take place in secret because it was feared that the pressure of Washington might discourage foreign investors.[11] The growing presence of foreign firms meant that, increasingly, Cuba had four different economies, a thriving black economy providing some 60 per cent of the population's basic food needs, an independent, enclave export sector, a hard currency consumer market open to those with dollars, and a nationalised economy marked by low productivity and severe rationing and reliant to a great extent on voluntary work.[12]

The contradictions generated by this kind of mixed economy did not help ordinary Cubans accept the worsening of their living conditions. As prices rose and supplies of basic commodities dwindled, living standards plummeted. Average calorie intake fell to 900 a day (compared to a norm of 2,500) and diseases associated with malnutrition and vitamin deficiency, banished from Cuba by the Revolution in 1959, began to re-appear. A new disease, Optical Neuritis, also spread and was only brought under control in September 1993. Ordinary Cubans had to suffer increasing power-cuts and reductions in public services, while for most, Chinese-made bicycles became the only means of private transport after drastic rationing of fuel (even the army had to parade on bikes on traditional patriotic celebrations). But the different opportunities offered by the mixed economy (some Cubans, for example, had easy access to dollars) served to erode the egalitarian basis of the Revolution and this in turn increasingly undermined the legitimacy of the regime itself. Even the privileged position enjoyed by the party and military elites was subverted by cuts; unlike the black marketeers and Cubans with generous relatives in exile in Miami, they had little access to dollars.[13] Cuba's continued achievements in health and education – with one of the best ratios of doctors per inhabitants and one of the lowest rates for infant mortality in the world – must have seemed to many Cubans poor compensation for the inadequacy of their diet and the absence of consumer goods. And the historical role which Castro had assigned Cubans of standing up to the US ('Our people know that on their shoulders rests a great historical responsibility . . .'[14]) was difficult to sustain when they were going hungry.

While they created fissures in Cuban society, the reforms did not challenge the basic model of the command economy. Besides, they were seen as piecemeal reforms arising out of the emergency created by the loss of the Soviet connection; as in time of war, economic decisions had to be improvised since no long-term planning was possible during the transition to new economic relationships. Though noticeably less energetic than before, Castro was once again in his element; emergencies had been the stuff of his career. Surrounded by his special group of advisors, he roamed the island, initiating inspired and sometimes less than inspired improvisations to problems of production and supply. Always susceptible to technological elixirs, he was prone to launch programmes that had been insufficiently tested, some of which appeared to fail or generated costs they were meant to avoid.[15]

Economic reform, therefore, was the product not so much of new thinking about the economic system as the regime's sheer need for survival. Aware of the contradictions of dollarisation, Castro introduced the measure on television (thereby breaking with the precedent of closed National Assembly deliberations) by stating, 'It hurts but we must be intelligent . . . and we have the right to invent things to survive in these conditions without ever ceasing to be revolutionaries.'[16] On the contrary, Castro continued to assert the regime's orthodoxy in the midst of a world-wide collapse of Soviet–style socialism. The slogan 'Socialism or Death', first coined at the beginning of 1989 on the thirtieth anniversary of the Revolution, became the rallying cry of all his speeches. And Castro never ceased to berate capitalism. Announcing the monetary reform measures package of January 1994, he declared, 'Authorising private commerce would be a political and ideological turnaround; it would be like starting along the path towards capitalism ... I find capitalism repugnant. It is filthy [una porquería], it is gross, it is alienating ... because it causes war, hypocrisy and competition'.[17]

Like the Chinese leadership's attempt to balance modernisation with authoritarian rule, Castro was trying to carry out a partial re-integration of the economy into the world market without significantly altering the internal order.[18] Far from encouraging reform, the collapse of Soviet and East European socialism reinforced his belief that any tinkering with the political system would have disastrous consequences. Though he felt Gorbachev had wanted to 'perfect' socialism, the Soviet leader's policies of *glasnost* and *perestroika* had undermined the legitimacy of the Communist Party. 'A process was unleashed', Castro said, referring to Gorbachev's reforms, 'which led to the destruction of the party's authority, and destroying the authority of the party meant destroying one of the pillars ... of socialism ...'. The disintegration of the Soviet Union was thus seen as a result of errors rather than of any systemic flaws.[19] In a speech to the National Assembly in March 1993, Castro lamented the consequences of the collapse of the former Soviet Union, 'What we are seeing is whole nations dying from disillusionment because of mediocre political illusions that were put into their heads ... Some of these former socialist countries don't know what they are or what they're going to do ... There is no plan, no order, no programme, there is nothing and what can come of nothing? What is left but frustration, misery, inequality, injustice?' Indeed, much was made in the state–controlled mass media, of the problems facing the people of the Commonwealth of Independent States as a result of the adoption of market reform and pluralism.[20]

The experience of the Sandinistas in Nicaragua, who had embraced social democracy and ended up losing the elections in February 1990, also suggested that any uncontrolled political *apertura* was too dangerous an experiment. While the US offensive against Cuba continued, any substantial political reform would be seen as weakness, encouraging

Washington to escalate its demands. Castro hinted that if the embargo were lifted and US–Cuban relations were normalised, 'another form of political leadership' might become possible, though he insisted that this would not be a bourgeois democracy.[21]

Yet in the wake of the corruption trials of 1989, when the leadership had launched a campaign of mass assemblies to shore up the legitimacy of the regime, it became clear that there was a groundswell of support for political reform and a partial liberalisation of the economy.[22] A reformist tendency emerged within the Party, one of whose more cautious exponents was the head of ideology and international relations, Carlos Aldana. Backed by intellectuals and some top administrators, the reformists advocated a number of significant reforms: limited political pluralism, including permission for opposition figures to stand in elections, partial economic reform, an independent media, a lay as opposed to an atheist state, and a return in the regime's propaganda to a stress on the national origins of the Revolution as opposed to its 'international socialist' credentials.[23] This was no programme of *perestroika* but it was enough to challenge the position of the more conservative sections of the Party and the leadership, who viewed any reform with suspicion in the light of events in Eastern Europe and the Soviet Union. Thus it was no surprise that Aldana was dropped from the leadership in autumn of 1992 and replaced by a more conservative man, an ex-ambassador to the Soviet Union, though the official explanation for Aldana's removal was that he had been involved in a financial scandal.[24]

The Congress, however, voted in favour of elements of the reformists' programme. The article in the Party's constitution committing it to atheism was removed, while the Party itself was partially re-defined to include its 'national character'. The Congress also approved the direct election of deputies to the National Assembly. These were not significant changes; while candidates for the Assembly could now be elected directly in a secret ballot, they had to be chosen as candidates by selection committees of the grass-roots organisations and while they need not be party members, no non-party organisation could put up candidates. Thus in the general elections of February 1993, 70 per cent of candidates were party members and all candidates, including two Protestant ministers who were eventually elected, were listed in the so-called 'united ballot' proposed by the government. The choice offered voters, therefore, was to vote for the official slate, abstain or spoil the ballot. In the event, with a turnout of 98.8 per cent, 88.4 per cent voted for the united ballot, 7.2 per cent spoilt the ballot and 4 per cent voted for only one candidate on the list.[25]

The purge of the reformists, therefore, did not signal a total rejection of reform. Sacking their leading proponents while appropriating some of their proposals was a way of acknowledging their ideas without allowing them to challenge the regime. Conversely, it satisfied conservative opponents of change within the party and the military without abandoning the possibility of limited reform. The action of the leadership suggested once again that Castro was not free to dictate policy but had constantly to balance conflicting interests within and outside the party.

Despite his rhetorical defence of socialist orthodoxy, however, Castro's speeches and interviews increasingly stressed a theme that had been constant throughout his political career: that the primary contradiction in the contemporary world was not between social classes but between North and South, between developed and developing nations. Cuban Socialism, a mix of centralism, austerity and social justice, was presented as a model not for industrialised economies, as in orthodox Marxist texts, but for Third World countries. In an interview in a Spanish magazine, he stated, 'Marx thought that socialism was the natural outcome of a developed capitalist society. But life has taught us that socialism is the ideal instrument of development in countries that have been left behind.' In a similar interview with a Mexican reporter in 1991, he said, 'They talk about the failure of socialism but where is the success of capitalism in Africa, Asia and Latin America?'[26] After the collapse of Soviet socialism, Castro set himself up even more emphatically as the champion of the world's poor against the post-Communist triumphalism of liberal capitalism. At the Fourth Congress, he declared, 'Now we have a universal responsibility . . . we are struggling not only for ourselves and our ideas, but for the ideas of all the exploited, subjugated, pillaged and hungry people in the world.'[27]

Nevertheless, the potential for solidarity among Third World countries had perhaps never been lower than in the mid-nineties. Cuba's erstwhile allies in Latin America and Africa had either lost power or had embraced the new capitalist orthodoxy. It was symptomatic that Castro's friend and the former socialist Prime Minister of Jamaica, Michael Manley, had been hired by Cable and Wireless to try to persuade the Cuban government to award the British firm a contract to modernise Cuba's telephone network.[28] Nevertheless, Castro still commanded widespread support in Latin America, as was evident in his visit to Bolivia and Colombia in the summer of 1993 during which he was besieged by crowds of well-wishers. He remained for many a symbol of defiance against the continued economic and cultural imperialism of the United States. But his old Bolivarian vision of a Latin America united against the predatory North behind tariff and debt barriers no longer held any charm for Latin American leaders who had renegotiated their debt problems and were keen to gain new credits and benefit from closer trading links with the United States.[29]

Cuba might have become once again an acceptable political partner in Latin America, having abandoned long ago its continental guerrilla strategy – Castro was welcomed by the Mexican President Carlos Salinas at the summit meeting of Latin American heads of state in Guadalajara (to which for the first time, the US was not invited) and the Caribbean common market (Caricom) was discussing trade with the Cuban government – but Cuba's policies and those of most Latin American leaders were going in opposite directions, as Castro himself recognised.[30] For its own part, the Latin American Left had abandoned the democratic centralist and state socialist model still espoused by Cuba, while the Panamerican anti-imperialist traditions of Lázaro Cárdenas and Perón were being radically re-defined by their heirs, Carlos Salinas and the President of Argentina, Carlos Menem. For the time being, Castro's attempt to invoke a radical, nationalist Latin American heritage could win him neither a new following in the continent nor a renewed legitimacy in Cuba.[31]

Similarly, since Rectification and in particular after the collapse of the Soviet Union, the Cuban leadership tended to play down analogies with the October Revolution in favour of the autocthonous origins of the Cuban Revolution and its Latin American connections.[32] The previous flow of articles about fraternal links with Eastern Europe and the Soviets gave way to columns about contemporary Latin America and the heroes of Latin American and Cuban independence. Socialism became a synonym for the peculiar nature of Cuban experience, though Cuban leaders continued to use the rhetoric of Marxism–Leninism. The works of Che Guevara, a fierce critic of Soviet revisionism, were once again promoted by Castro. 'My admiration and my sympathy for Che have grown', said Castro in an interview in 1992, 'as I have seen everything that has occurred in the socialist camp, because he was firmly opposed to the methods of building socialism using the categories of capitalism.'[33] In the February 1993 elections to the National Assembly, Castro himself stood as a candidate in a constituency at the foot of the Sierra Maestra which included some of the suburbs of Santiago; it was a symbolic gesture, helping to evoke the early days of the Revolution. Alongside the ponderous dogma of Soviet socialism, Castro renewed the Guevarist appeal to justice and egalitarianism as the essential categories of the Revolution. Thus in his last years as leader, Castro reached back to the early values of the Revolution before his adoption of Marxism–Leninism.

Castro's continued legitimacy among Cubans rested above all on his appeal to beleaguered nationalism. The victory of the Democrats in the 1992 US elections did not lessen the American offensive against Cuba, despite Castro's optimism about Bill Clinton's intentions.[34] The Cuban Democracy Act (otherwise known as the Torricelli Amendment) of November 1992, giving the US President powers to ban all US subsidiaries, based in third countries, from trading with Cuba, had been promoted by a Democrat and supported by Clinton himself, though twice the United Nations voted by an overwhelming majority against the US embargo of Cuban trade. Castro's demands for ever greater sacrifices by the Cuban people could be justified by the 'blockade' of Cuba and political centralisation legitimised by the sense of siege. The same feelings of insecurity had led to the creation of vigilante groups or Rapid Response Brigades of volunteers in 1991 to counter a potential fifth column; more often than not they were employed to harass representatives of Cuban human rights organisations or individuals demanding political reform.

After the collapse of the Soviet Union most non-Cuban commentators were confidently predicting the imminent collapse of Castro's regime. But his continued survival into the mid-nineties should not have come as a surprise. There was no organised opposition to the regime in Cuba because it was not allowed and any attempt to muster collective criticism of its policies was severely repressed. The army remained the most powerful institution in Cuba and the loyalty of the top echelon of officers to Castro was unquestionable. The price of discordance with the leadership was high; among the accusations against General Ochoa in his trial in 1989 was that he had shown signs of 'populism' though there was no evidence that he had had any popular support. And Castro had always been careful to maintain an equilibrium between the different 'families' of the regime to ensure unity and to forestall any challenge to the regime. But as the living conditions of Cubans further declined, the political situation became more volatile. By the mid-nineties, Castro's Revolution still hung in the balance.

. . .

NOTES AND REFERENCES

1. Mesa-Lago C (ed.) 1993 *Cuba after the Cold War*. University of Pittsburgh, p. 151
2. Quirk R E 1994 *Fidel Castro*. Norton, New York, p. 832
3. *Latin American Weekly Report*, 12 Sept. 1991
4. *Latinoamericana Press*, 30 Sept. 1993
5. *The Guardian*, 22 Feb. 1992; *Granma International*, 28 March 1993
6. In an interview with Tomás Borge 1992 *Un grano de maíz, conversación con Fidel Castro*. Fondo de Cultura Económica, Mexico, pp. 178–9
7. Mesa-Lago 1993 pp. 165–7
8. Op. cit., pp. 227–44
9. 'Keeping the Faith', *The Economist*, 9 Oct. 1993
10. Lydia Larifla 1993 'Fin du CAEM et sous-développement dévoilé à Cuba', *Problèmes d'Amérique Latine* n. 10 July–Sept. 1993, pp. 40–1, *Latinamerica Press*, 30 Sept. 1993
11. Mesa-Lago 1993 p. 202

12. *Latin American News Service*, week ending 18 Feb. 1994; Larifla 1993 p. 50; Jorge I. Domínguez, 'Cuba's Switch from State Economy', *The Financial Times*, 26 Jan. 1994
13. *Economist*, 9 Oct. 1993. A CIA spokesman, appearing before the US Senate's Intelligence Committee in July 1993, argued that the legalisation of the dollar would 'aggravate social tensions and distinctions in Cuba because only a small proportion of the population will receive hard currency from overseas': *Caribbean and Central America Report*, 26 Aug. 1993
14. Borge 1992 p. 194
15. Mesa-Lago (1993 pp. 234–8) refers to several recent examples among which are the substitution of liquid fodder for imported grain for feeding pigs and the mass production of a locally invented multiplow
16. *Latin American Weekly Report*, 15 July 1993
17. Op. cit., 13 Jan. 1994
18. A number of top officials were sent to China to study the effect of economic reforms there: *Caribbean and Central America Report*, 27 Jan. 1994
19. Borge 1992 p. 48; *Granma International*, 5 May 1991
20. Castro quote from *Reuter*, 16 March 1993; *New York Times*, 13 Jan. 1993
21. Borge 1992 p. 120
22. Marifeli Pérez-Stable 1992 'Charismatic Authority, Vanguard Party Politics and Popular Mobilizations: Revolution and Socialism in Cuba', *Cuban Studies*, vol. 22 1992, p. 19
23. *Latin American Weekly Report*, op. cit.
24. *New York Times*, 12 Oct. 1992; *Financial Times*, 26–27 Sept. 1992. The official explanation was that Aldana had been guilty of 'deficiencies in his work and serious errors of a personal nature in the fulfilment of his duties'. For further details see *Granma International*, 18 Oct. 1992
25. *Economist*, 6 March 1993; official figures gave a 99.62 per cent turnout and only 3.05 per cent blank votes and 3.9 per cent spoilt ballots
26. *Cambio 16*, 25 June 1990; *Siempre*, 30 May 1991
27. Reed G 1992 *Island in the Storm. The Cuban Communist Party's Fourth Congress.* Ocean Press, Melbourne, p. 32
28. *Financial Times*, 25 Nov. 1993; *Caribbean and Central America Report*, 27 Jan. 1994. In the event, the deal fell through, perhaps as a result of US pressure

29. *Reuter*, 9 Aug. 1993. Castro had also attempted to appeal to the Presidents of Mexico, Colombia and Venezuela in 1991 in an unscheduled visit to Cozumel where they were meeting. He had come back empty-handed, having been told that Cuba could not be admitted to regional trade pacts until it carried out substantive political and economic reforms.
30. Borge 1992 p. 160
31. Rhoda Rabkin 1992 'Cuban Socialism: Ideological Responses to the Era of Socialist Crisis' *Cuban Studies* no. 22, p. 29
32. A typical example is Armando Hart's article 'A Battle for the Identity of Our America' in *Granma International*, 18 April 1993
33. Borge 1992 pp. 80–1
34. During the July 1993 summit of Latin American leaders in Brazil, Castro declared 'It seems to me that Clinton belongs to another generation of Americans . . . I have the impression he's a decent person and a peaceful one.' *AP*, 5 Aug. 1993

Chapter 10

SITTING ON THE SEAWALL

This book can have no concluding chapter. While he is still alive and vigorous, Castro and not his biographers will have the last word. For all the problems he has had to face since the collapse of the Soviet Union, he remains the unchallenged leader of the Cuban state. From any standpoint, his survival is an extraordinary feat. Despite the unswerving hostility of the most powerful country in the world situated less than 90 miles away (or 90 millimetres, as Castro has said jokingly), his regime has remained afloat and implemented policies that have defied Washington. It has achieved a degree of development in social infrastructure that surpasses that of most countries in Latin America. These successes have been due in great measure to Castro's ability to tap the creative energies of millions of Cubans in defence of a hundred-year-old aspiration for national independence. After more than thirty-five years in power, however, Castro is still as far as ever from achieving the utopian goals that he set in the Moncada programme and in the heady days of revolutionary triumph. Cuba has been unable to break out of its economic dependence and is indeed now poised on the edge of economic disaster.

The Cuban Revolution was an authentic response to the problems of underdevelopment and neo-colonial dependency by a nationalist elite drawn mainly from the middle class and backed by popular support. Despite the labels it has attached to itself, the Revolution was essentially part of the wave of anti-colonial struggles in the Third World during the post-war period led by disaffected or disenfranchised members of the educated urban middle class such as Nasser, Nkrumah, Nyerere and Ben Bella. As in Cuba, the driving force of these movements was the need to achieve economic as well as national independence through modernisation. Because many of its leaders came from a class closely bound up with the state (military officers or lawyers for example) the new regime tended to see the state as the fundamental instrument for the transformation of society. In order to overthrow the colonial or neo-colonial regimes, the new elite had to mobilise the popular masses around a programme of social reform as well as national self-assertion. Political and economic centralisation in one degree or another was in many cases unavoidable because of internal contradictions or external pressures, for example from the ex-colonial powers. Such pressures often led to a political alignment with the Soviet bloc. Thus a centralised state, a more or less nationalised economy and populist base became the hallmarks of many post-colonial governments, and, because of this formal resemblance to socialism, the doctrines on which they were based were called socialist when in fact their main inspiration was indigenous; hence the emergence of Islamic or African 'socialism'.

A closer source from which Castro drew inspiration was the Latin American anti-imperialist movements of the thirties and forties. During the Great Depression, new political movements had emerged, as in Mexico, Argentina and Brazil, which sought to break out of the cycle of dependence on the export of traditional cash crops or raw materials by modernising the economy. To do so, they had mobilised mass movements both to wrest political control from the traditional elites whose rule had rested on command of the export economy and also to destroy the hegemony of American economic interests. Of these movements, the most influential in the Latin American continent had been that of Perón in Argentina. As a student, Che Guevara had been a supporter of Perón, and Castro himself took part, as we have seen, in the anti-imperialist student congress in Colombia in 1947 which was sponsored by Perón. Other populist Latin American leaders who could be said to have influenced Castro included the immensely popular Colombian politician Jorge Gaitán, whose assassination sparked off the riots that Castro joined in 1947, and Colonel Jacobo Arbenz, whose attempt to carry out land reform as President of Guatemala was cut short by an American-sponsored armed invasion in 1954, witnessed by Che Guevara and no doubt recounted at length to Castro when he met him shortly afterwards in Mexico.

The main source of the inspiration and legitimacy of Castro's Revolution, however, has been the Cuban nationalist tradition in its more radical version. Castro saw his own movement as the culmination of a time-honoured struggle for independence and development stretching from the first revolt against colonial rule in 1868 to the student rebellion of the thirties. His own supreme self-confidence was based on the conviction that he embodied that struggle. Indeed, there has been an underlying consistency in Castro's beliefs that belies his apparently abrupt change from regenerationism to Marxism–Leninism. Though he claims to have effected a juncture between Martí and Marx, the values that have guided him throughout his political career have in fact been drawn above all from Cuban and Spanish traditions. The vein of moral regeneration and voluntarism that runs through his political thought has much more in common with Hispanic nationalism than with European socialism or Soviet Communism.

The Cuban regime's official adoption of Marxism–Leninism was motivated not merely by expediency but by the belief held by Castro and other leaders of the Revolution that it offered the only possible model of economic growth and the only international movement with which they could identify. But this was also because there were elements of Marxism that merged with ideas transmitted through the Cuban radical tradition. The two most important of these were the notion of proletarian international solidarity, translated in the Cuban version into solidarity with the 'poor and oppressed peoples' of the world, and a teleological faith in the inevitability of progress or, in its Marxist version, of socialism.

In its journey to Cuba, just as in its other Third World appearances, the content of Marxism was transformed. Indigenous populist traditions became absorbed by Marxist–Leninist terminology and translated into new categories: people became proletariat, nation became class, and nationalism became socialism. But the experience of the Cuban Revolution hardly squared with the Marxist axiom that it was the class struggle which created the conditions for socialism. On the contrary, the Revolution was led largely by a middle-class elite claiming to act on behalf of the people. Despite his claim that a 'people's government' came to power in 1959, Castro has also repeatedly stressed that the masses were not ready to assume government. 'The people', he argued in an interview in 1985, 'had to be led to the road of revolution by stages, step by step, until they achieved full political awareness and confidence in their future'.[1] Workers had been tainted by the experience of capitalism, according to this view, and the revolutionary leadership had to ensure the development of their socialist consciousness. As Castro readily admitted during his tour of Chile in 1971, 'We have been working on building our workers' movement.'[2] Similarly, in a speech to the Ministry of the Interior in 1986, he attacked the abuse of material incentives, claiming that it 'corrupts nothing less than those whose consciousness we are obliged to preserve'.[3] Hence labour problems such as absenteeism and low productivity have been seen as the result not of any contradiction between workers and the new state claiming to act on their behalf, but of old habits or new forms of corporatism. The Marxist notion of working-class power is absent from Castro's thinking; it means for him either 'selfishness' or the 'demagogic and criminal' ideas of Yugoslav–style self-management.[4]

Indeed, in Castro's political theory, socialism was not so much a question of power as one of distribution. As in other Third World countries that hoisted the socialist banner, it was articulated as an egalitarian philosophy whose main component was the welfare state. In this sense, Castro assimilated some of the classical values of European socialism, values that were embedded in any case in Cuba's radical traditions. Societies were defined as socialist also if their states owned the means of production. Castro was thus able to describe China as socialist in an interview in 1977 even though he considered its foreign policy reactionary: 'China is socialist but it is not internationalist . . . I believe China is a socialist country because there are no landlords nor capitalists there.'[5] The apparent contradiction between China's domestic and foreign policies stemmed from a 'deformation' of socialism on the part of its leaders, as if the two practices could be autonomous from one another.

In fact, Castro's definition of China reflected his own conception of state policy as the preserve of a political leadership free to conduct government affairs without excessive control from below and therefore able to change course virtually at will. The structures of popular participation set up in 1976 did not shift power from the leadership to the people but created channels through which popular demands could rise to the top and directives from above could flow down to the people. Power still remained in practice in the hands of a small group of leaders, though these had to be responsive to the interests of the different elites.

The political dimension of Castro's authoritarianism sprang from three main sources: the formative experiences of imprisonment on the Isle of Pines, and of the guerrilla struggle, in which military hierarchy and obedience had been necessary for survival; an elitist belief that only the loyal and battle-hardened leaders could be trusted to steer the Revolution in the right direction; and the conviction that in the conditions of siege and scarcity there was no room for pluralism in the style of Western democracy. The Bay of Pigs invasion had burned the old fear of the United States on the psyche of the Cuban leaders, so much so that anti-Americanism became almost the raison d'être of the Revolution, just as, with far less justification, 'communist subversion' in Central America and the Caribbean became an obsession of Washington.

To understand the lure of authoritarianism in Cuba, the full extent of America's offensive against Cuba has to be taken into account. According to US Senate reports, the CIA's second largest station in the world was based in Florida. From here, just across the water from Cuba, it ran up to 120,000 Cuban agents, who dealt in economic sabotage, assassination and terrorism, and controlled an airline and a flotilla of spy ships operating off the coast of Cuba.[6] Some 500 hours of anti-Castro propaganda were broadcast weekly from radio stations in Florida. Successive US governments, in particular the Reagan administration, have mobilised their most powerful resources to bring Cuba to its knees.

Political centralisation and repression in Cuba, therefore, were a response to a deep sense of national insecurity rather than to the dictates of an ageing leader clinging to power. In Castro's eyes, the life-or-death struggle to defend the new Cuba and build its economy required discipline and austerity,

179

not political and cultural pluralism. This conviction coloured his response to events elsewhere. Just as he disapproved of the Prague Spring of 1968, so he condemned the student protest in Tiananmen Square. The Cuban press reported only the official Chinese version of what happened, and the Cuban government sent an undivulged message of support to the Chinese leaders after the massacre.[7]

The continued centralisation of political life in the hands of a small elite, however, has created a habit of deference and passivity. Without a radical renewal of leadership from below, it is difficult to see how Castro could easily be replaced. Now in his late sixties, broader round the middle, his beard gone grey and his movements slower, Castro seems to have lost little of his energy, his voracity for knowledge and his elephantine memory. He continues to astound visitors with his erudition; he can and does talk for hours about a wide variety of subjects ranging from the latest developments in biotechnology to cheese biscuits. He is a gourmet cook and an accomplished scuba-diver. Such is the continued fear of his assassination, according to an article in a Russian newspaper, that nearly 10,000 bodyguards are assigned to protect him, including 100 divers who comb the sea-bed for mines when he goes swimming.[8]

Castro seems to have embraced power and held on to it with an unshakeable sense of historical mission. Asked by an American interviewer in 1985 whether he felt lonely, he answered that he didn't because he felt he was 'among the people'. However, he went on, 'I can feel some of the bitterness of power, the sacrifices that come with power, having to submit to that torture ... At times one feels the need to do things everybody else does, simple, ordinary things: sit on the seawall [the popular *Malecón* along Havana's sea-front], go somewhere, things I cannot do. But for a long time now I have come to accept this way of life and it doesn't make me unhappy'.[9] As the regime faced ever increasing pressures to compromise its values, the taste of power doubtless got more bitter. Just out of sight of the *Malecón*, a Cuban tourist ship with a casino now regularly plies up and down and along the road to the seaside resort of Varadero neon-lit signboards advertise Cuban rum.

Castro hinted in 1993 that he might retire if and when the Special Period came to an end. 'Time goes by', he said in an interview during the elections, 'and even marathon runners get tired. My race has been a long one, with marvellous experiences but very long and there are other compañeros who can do it as well as me . . . I hope my compañeros do not demand [that I should run again in elections] and that by then the difficult conditions of the Special Period may have disappeared . . .'[10] But the dilemma facing the regime was that it could not afford to let Castro retire and sit on the seawall, even if he were really willing to do so. Without him, it would be difficult to demand continuing sacrifices from the Cubans. The pivot of the regime is Castro, in whose image it has been created and sustained. It is Castro on the whole who has held together the disparate elements of Cuban society, the masses and the elites, the young and the old, the black and the white. Popular images of Castro vary, from the all-Cuban hero, the daring tough-talking man of the people who faced up to the Americans, to the solicitous and incorruptible patriarch. He is also seen by other Cubans as a ranting old greybeard and by some as a tyrant. The fact that politics in Cuba is so often refracted through the image of one man means that any criticism is an implicit attack on Castro himself. The opportunities for democratic debate and decision-making have been diminished by his continued moral and political hegemony.

Some of the orthodox panegyrics upon Castro imply that the Revolution was due largely to his leadership. Castro has been the first to decry such simplistic versions of history.[11] It is true he has displayed extraordinary qualities that account in some measure for his successes. Among these have been his dogged persistence in the face of intolerable odds, his luck (if that can be described as a quality), courage, integrity, ability as a facilitator of ideas without being a particularly original thinker himself, and ideological flexibility in pursuit of strategic goals. Yet Castro's early personal triumph derived largely from the peculiar historical conditions that existed in Cuba in the fifties. He owed his success equally to his identification with the old nationalist vision of his country. The Revolution was the latest link in a chain of events in Cuba that began with an uprising against Spanish colonial rule. While it is unthinkable without him, it followed a path laid down by many earlier unsuccessful attempts to achieve independence. Castro remade history but he did so with tools inherited from Cuba's past. For all his apparent swings of policy and diversity of ideologies, there is a continuity in Castro's political ideas which has its origins in the hundred-year-old, and still unfinished, struggle for independence and development. It is this aspiration on the part of millions of Cubans as much as his own qualities as a political leader that account for his remarkable career.

· · ·

NOTES AND REFERENCES

1. Betto F 1987 *Fidel and Religion*. Weidenfeld and Nicolson, London, p. 149
2. Castro Ruz F 1972 *Fidel in Chile*. International Publishers, New York, p. 131
3. *Granma*, 8 June 1986
4. Castro Ruz 1972 pp. 15 and 131
5. Castro F 1977 *Fidel Castro habla con Barbara Walters*. Carlos Valencia Editores, Colombia, p. 68
6. Didion J 1987 *Miami*. Weidenfeld and Nicolson, London, pp. 90–1; Hinckle W and Turner W W 1981 *The Fish is Red. The Story of the Secret War against Castro*. Harper and Row, New York
7. This was confirmed to the author by the Chinese Press Attaché in London. For the Cuban press response see *Granma Weekly Review (GWR)*, 18 June 1989. See also Castro's comments on CNN quoted in Mesa-Lago 1993 p. 200
8. He is also reported to have 3 yachts and some 30 safe-houses: reported in the *Evening Standard*, 27 Nov. 1990 from *Komsomolskaya Pravda*, 18 Oct. 1990
9. NBC interview quoted in *GWR*, 13 March 1985
10. *Latin America Weekly Report*, 11 March 1993
11. For example, Castro F 1986 *Nothing can Stop the Course of History*. Pathfinder, New York, p. 23

BIBLIOGRAPHICAL ESSAY

Books in English

Very little of Castro's written work has appeared in English. Selected articles and speeches from the period up to the triumph of the Revolution are published in 1972 *Revolutionary Struggle 1947–1958*, Cambridge, MA. Similarly, only a tiny proportion of Castro's prolific output as an orator has been translated into English. Although repetitive at times, these speeches are an important source for understanding his ideas and discourse. Three collections are published by Harvester Press: M Taber 1981, 1983 *Fidel Castro Speeches* and *In Defence of Socialism*, 1989. Selected speeches appear in M Kenner and J Petras (eds) 1970 *Fidel Castro Speaks*, Allen Lane, London. His speech at the Moncada trial appears in 1968 *History Will Absolve Me*, Jonathan Cape, London, while selected speeches made during his tour of Chile in 1971 appear in 1972 *Fidel in Chile*, International Publishers, New York. An invaluable collection of letters and documents of the Sierra campaign is contained in C Franqui 1980 *Diary of the Cuban Revolution*, Viking Press, New York.

Two lengthy interviews with Castro have appeared in English in recent years; by far the more interesting is his interview with the Brazilian theologian Frei Betto 1987 *Fidel and Religion*, Simon & Schuster, New York, during which Castro clearly warmed to his interviewer and spoke at some length about his childhood and youth, as well as giving his views on Christianity and Marxism and the problem of Third World debt. The second interview, also of considerable interest, was conducted in 1985 by the black Democratic Congressman Mervyn M Dymally and his foreign affairs adviser: Fidel Castro *Nothing Can Stop the Course of History*, Pathfinder, New York.

Two recent biographies of Castro contain some useful insights. The first, Peter Bourne 1987 *Castro*, Macmillan, London, is a somewhat maverick portrait by a psychiatrist and former adviser to President Carter, marred slightly by an over-emphasis on Castro's allegedly problematic relationship with his father as a driving force of his actions. The second is a more balanced account by an American journalist who has followed Castro's career for many years and was able to interview him at length (though, according to Castro himself, he was not officially given the wide facilities that he claims): Tad Szulc 1987 *Fidel: a Critical Portrait*, Hutchinson, London. Szulc's book contains a wealth of personal detail and Castro's own observations but, like Bourne's biography, deals cursorily with the last twenty-five years or so, a period as important and as fascinating as the early years. Both are relatively lightweight in terms of their analysis of the ideological or historical context. More recently, two further biographies of Castro have appeared, Georgie Anne Geyer 1991 *Guerrilla Prince. The Untold Story of Fidel Castro*, Little, Brown, Toronto, and Robert E. Quirk 1993 *Fidel Castro*, W W Norton, New York. The first is too deeply informed by Cold War perspectives to offer any new insights and while the second is thoroughly documented, both are so relentlessly hostile towards Castro that they fail to convince.

Of books published earlier that deal with or touch on Castro's role in the Revolution, several are worthy of mention. The ex-editor of the 26th July Movement's newspaper, Carlos Franqui, who was to have been Castro's official biographer until he left Cuba in protest at the turn to Communism, has written an uneven and impressionistic account of the Cuban leader, the effect of which is somewhat spoiled by his visceral opposition to Castro: 1983 *Family Portrait with Fidel*, Random House, New York. The same is true of the book of another 26th July leader, Mario Llerena 1978 *The Unsuspected Revolution: the Birth and Rise of Castroism*, Cornell University Press, Ithaca, NY, though it contains interesting details and documents concerning the external relations of the Movement. A more balanced though critical account of Castro in the sixties can be found in K S Karol 1970 *Guerrillas in Power: the Course of the Cuban*

Revolution, Hill & Wang, New York, and in the analysis of the French agronomist, René Dumont 1974 *Is Cuba Socialist?* Viking Press, New York, one of many European intellectuals whose support for the Revolution turned sour in the late sixties. A sympathetic and interesting portrait of Castro as a young man appears in Lionel Martin 1978 *The. Early Fidel: Roots of Castro's Communism*, Lyle Stuart, Seacaucus, NJ, though he overstates both the ideological debt the youthful Castro owed to Communist ideas and the working-class base of the 26th July Movement in the early fifties. Hugh Thomas's encyclopaedic work on the history of Cuba: 1971 *Cuba: the Pursuit of Freedom*, Harper & Row, New York, is by far the most complete study of the historical background of the Revolution but is less satisfactory as an examination of Castro's political ideas and strategies.

Books dealing with the Revolution itself are legion. Only a few need to be mentioned here for the light they throw on Castro. The most serious accounts are the academic monographs published by American universities specialising in Cuban studies, among which the following stand out: Jorge I Domínguez 1978 *Cuba: Order and Revolution*, Harvard University Press, Cambridge, MA; Carmelo Mesa-Lago 1974 *Cuba in the 1970s: Pragmatism and Institutionalization*, University of New Mexico; Edward Gonzalez 1974 *Cuba under Castro: the Limits of Charisma*, Houghton Mifflin, Boston; Andrew Zimbalist (ed.) 1988 *Cuban Political Economy: Controversies in Cubanology*, Westview Press, Boulder, CO. Wayne S Smith's *The Closest of Enemies* 1987, W W Norton, New York, contains some interesting inside analysis of Cuban–American relations during the Carter administration and the early years of Reagan's presidency. Also worthy of inclusion in this list of more general works are three more recent books: Max Azicri 1988 *Cuba: Politics, Economics and Society*, Pinter Publishers, London: Louis A Pérez Jr. 1988 *Cuba: Between Reform and Revolution*, Oxford University Press, New York; and Jean Stubbs 1989 *Cuba: the Test of Time*, Latin American Bureau, London.

. . .

Books in Spanish

Many of Castro's speeches have been published in Cuba. A recent collection of these covering the years 1986–7 can be

CASTRO

found in Fidel Castro 1988 *Por el Camino Correcto*, Editora Política, Havana. Of interest also are his interviews with Barbara Walters of the NBC: 1977 *Fidel Castro habla con Barbara Walters*, Carlos Valencia, Colombia; with American and French journalists in 1983 *Conversaciones con periodistas norteamericanos y franceses*, Editora Política, Havana; and with the Mexican daily paper, *Excelsior*, published in 1985 by the Editora Política: *La cancelación de la deuda externa y el nuevo orden económico internacional como única alternativa verdadera*. The Italian TV journalist Gianni Minà has published the transcript of his interview with Castro: 1988 *Il racconto di Fidel*, Mondadori, Milan, and it provides some fascinating personal details about the Cuban leader. Correspondence between Castro and his friends and collaborators during his imprisonment on the Isle of Pines is published in Luis Conte Agüero 1959 *Cartas del Presidio*, Editorial Lex, Havana, while documents and details about the Moncada assault can be found in Marta Rojas 1964 *La generación del Centenario en el Moncada*, Ediciones R, Havana. A more complete collection of documents dealing with the early fifties is published in Mario Mencía 1986 *El Grito de Moncada*, 2 vols, Editora Política. Mencía has set out to write a lengthy journalistic description of the Cuban Revolution of which the above are part and 1986 *Tiempos Precursores*, Editorial de Ciencias Sociales, Havana, an accompanying volume. Like many semi-official histories of the Revolution, his books tend to be a hagiography of Castro; indeed, judging by some of the textbooks published by the Ministry of Higher Education in Cuba there is a lack of any serious analysis of the Revolution in some official circles, though this is not true, on the other hand, of the research being carried out in the universities by academics such as Oscar Pino Santos, Manuel Moreno Fraginals, Jorge Ibarra, and Olga Cabrera.

If the Cuban books on Castro tend to be hagiographies, the portraits of him by Cubans in exile are more in the way of demonologies. He is a legendary hero on the one hand and a power-hungry opportunist on the other, and there is little published in Spanish that occupies a middle ground. Two books by exiles can be mentioned as examples: José Pardo Llada 1988 *Fidel y el 'Che'*, Plaza y Janés, Barcelona; and Carlos Alberto Montaner 1984 *Fidel Castro y la Revolución Cubana*, Plaza y Janés. The first is the more interesting as it is written by a former friend and collaborator of Castro in the forties and fifties who became a Ortodoxo leader and a well-known radio and TV journalist in Havana before joining Castro in the Sierra in 1958. Though it contains some interesting anecdotes, his portrait of Castro as a wild, obsessively ambitious, and ideologically unsound young man reveals more about the author's bitterness at the supposed betrayal of the liberal cause of the revolutionary movement than it does about the ideas and character of the Cuban leader. It suggests once more the powerful hold that Castro continues to exercise on the imagination of Cubans, whether friends or foes.

MAPS

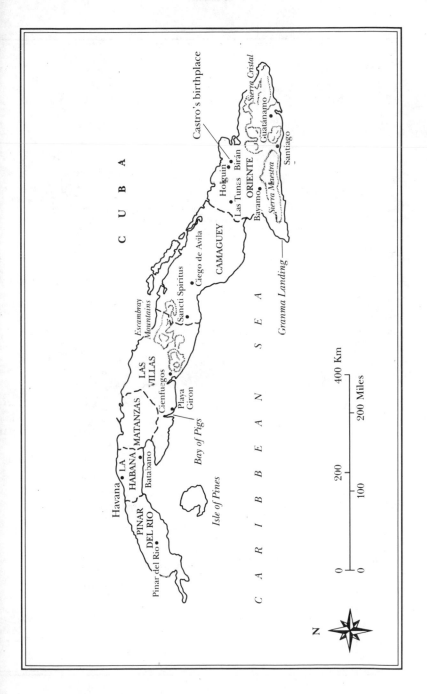

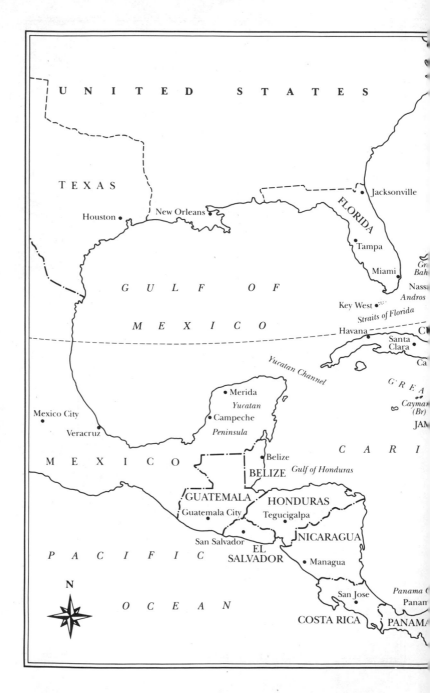

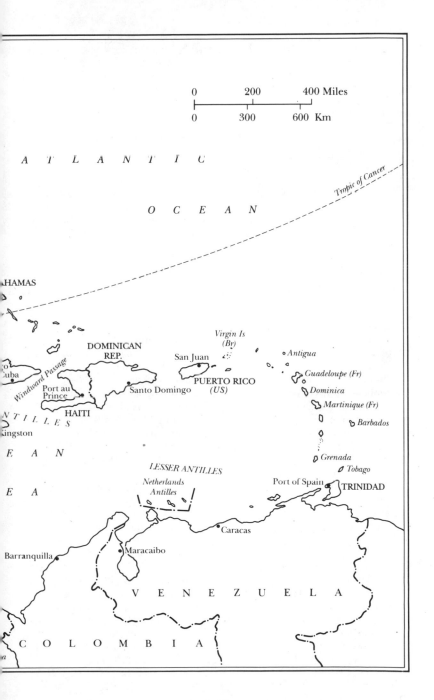

INDEX